dinner at your door

dinner at your door

TIPS AND RECIPES FOR STARTING A NEIGHBORHOOD COOKING CO-OP

ALEX DAVIS, DIANA ELLIS, ANDY REMEIS

PHOTOGRAPHS BY DEBORAH HARDEE

GIBBS SMITH
TO ENRICH AND INSPIRE HUMANKIND

Salt Lake City | Charleston | Santa Fe | Santa Barbara

First Edition
12 11 10 09 08   5 4 3 2 1

Published by
Gibbs Smith
P.O. Box 667
Layton, Utah 84041

Orders: 1.800.835.4993
www.gibbs-smith.com

Designed by Kristy Weyhrich, W Design
Printed and bound in China

Library of Congress Cataloging-in-Publication Data

Davis, Alex, cook.
    Dinner at your door : tips and recipes for starting a neighborhood cooking co-op / Alex Davis, Diana Ellis, Andy Remeis ; photographs by Deborah Hardee. — 1st ed.
        p. cm.
    Includes index.
    ISBN-13: 978-1-4236-0291-0
    ISBN-10: 1-4236-0291-9
    1. Dinners and dining. I. Ellis, Diana, cook. II. Remeis, Andy. III. Title.
    TX737.D34 2008
    641.5—dc22
                                        2008011557

To Mom & Dad FOR SHOWING ME HOW TO COOK WITH LOVE AND TO MICHAEL FOR ALL THE REST

—DIANA

For Paul & Jesse, Mom & Dad THANK YOU FOR BEING WHO YOU ARE IN MY LIFE

—ANDY

For my mom, Monica, WHO COOKS WITH THE EXCITEMENT OF A LITTLE KID

—ALEX

Contents

1 | Why Start a Dinner Co-op?

A LIFE OF LEISURE AND GOURMET CUISINE

WHAT IS A DINNER CO-OP?

A scheduling trick that will transform your life

A dinner co-op is a geographically close circle of cooks who alternate preparing and delivering fresh, hot weeknight meals so you get more than you give. The goal is to feed three or four households with just a bit more effort than it takes to feed one—and to feed them well.

It's essentially a logistical trick to reduce your responsibility during the week without compromising the family dinner hour or the quality of the meals you serve.

Co-ops aren't a new idea—throughout history, people have always teamed up to solve life's big challenges. Whether it was pitching in to build shelter, harvest crops, or defend from danger, communities were formed by the necessity of shared labor. Unlike those villagers, we aren't fighting fires with buckets of water from the well. We're just cranking out great homemade dinners and sharing them.

The dinner co-op is an essential lifestyle upgrade that has saved our sanity, challenged our creativity, and elevated our own cooking in ways we never thought possible. Along the way, it's become our foundation for a happy life.

RELAX LIKE A SLACKER, PRESENT LIKE A CHEF

Have your cake and bake it, too

Is it possible to spend nearly an entire workweek slacking off between 5:00 and 7:00 p.m.—the so-called "crunch time" in most households?

You bet it is. Form a neighborhood dinner co-op and gleefully abandon your mealtime responsibilities for the majority of the week. Work, goof off, or play with your kids all afternoon. Then simply answer the doorbell to hot, fresh, homemade dinners night after night.

And when it's your night to shine, go for it. No compromises—buy the good stuff at the store and adhere to classic cooking techniques. On your co-op night, you're no longer in survival mode. You've been saving your energy all week for this moment, so storm the kitchen on purpose. Take your time, enjoy yourself, and make something delicious. We'll show you how.

SO **THIS** IS BALANCE

Independence is a trap—interdependence is bliss

Remember your glorious early and mid-twenties? They were all about being independent. If the dinner hour came and went with only a handful of nachos, nobody was hurt by it but ourselves! But try pulling the same stunt with a child and two adults who need real fuel at the end of the day.

Anyone with kids or a demanding job quickly learns that independence equals exhaustion. Knowing you can't possibly do it all, perhaps you lean on friends for carpooling and play dates. Or maybe you've found room in the budget for lawn care or housekeeping to preserve what little free time you have. In every aspect of our lives, we're looking for solutions to give us a higher return on our time. Interdependence is the answer.

What would you do with an extra hour right after work? Maybe you have secret fantasies in which you finish reading the newspaper, try that new yoga/spin class, have a quiet glass of

BUILD YOUR DREAM SCHEDULE

	MONDAY	TUESDAY	WEDNESDAY	THURSDAY
4 pm to 6 pm	make dinner for the co-op	yoga	coffee date	read my novel

Tuesday night is yoga class, Wednesdays I meet my sister for coffee or give myself permission to do nothing! After having so many nights off to putter around or exercise, I look forward to the night set aside to cook a nutritious meal for my dinner co-op.

–Diana

wine with your partner, take a quick run through the neighborhood, finger paint with the kids, or take a hot bath.

Bring those longings out into the open! Partner with your friends and neighbors, use your "prepaid" time to forget about making dinner, and become the balanced person you want to be.

TAKE BACK THE DINING ROOM
Stay in and embrace the family dinner table

Regular people are spending untold sums building fantastic kitchens with the finest tools and equipment, striving to create the ultimate "heart" for their homes. Once we've spent enough money on our kitchen, we reason, our family will surely thrive.

But deep down we know there's only one thing that can guarantee thriving relationships, and it's not granite or stainless steel. It's *time* together. We need time to share the day we've had. Time to make eye contact, to listen, and to figure out what's going on with our partners and kids so we can help or adjust accordingly. In short, we need more time to be there for each other.

The most practical, traditional way to connect every night is at the dinner table. A dinner co-op hands it to you on a silver platter, bringing you structure and predictability to make dinner together a nightly routine. Without the stress of cooking and cleanup, it's easy to get in the mood to have a few laughs. Through no effort of your own, dinner arrives like clockwork at a specified time, hot and ready to eat. All that's left now is to sit down together and let the magic happen.

A GREENER WAY TO EAT YOUR GREENS
Protecting the planet, one dinner at a time

Imagine a residential block with a single oven on instead of four. Three or four families, only one trip to the market. No takeout containers, plastic bags, or credit card receipts from the restaurant. Just hot food made from scratch, sent out in a glass dish.

Kids running, riding bikes, or pulling a wagon to help deliver the carefully prepared meals. Neighbors and friends teaming up weekly for a simple, common sense endeavor that runs mostly on human power.

It doesn't take an environmentalist to see that neighborhood dinner co-ops are a smart, earth-friendly practice you can feel good about.

> **From the Neighborhood**
>
> If you think about your planet, your community, your family, and what you eat, then you are ready to form a dinner co-op.
>
> **—Paul on E. State Street**

2 | Finding Your Chefs

IDENTIFY A CIRCLE OF GREAT COOKS,
AND THE RESULTS WILL DAZZLE YOU

TRY BEFORE YOU BUY

Recruitment strategies

Consider the elements of a book club—women, wine, and food. Month after month, members may bring appetizers, salads, soups, and desserts to the meeting. A low-key way to "audition" chefs for your dinner co-op is to make a mental note when someone is clearly a good cook. From being in the club together, you may already share mutual trust, understanding, and a bit of history.

Expand this idea to any group that's loosely headquartered in your neighborhood. Are you in a neighborhood association? A dinner or movie club? Have any tennis or golf buddies? Consider parents you've met at school or on your kid's sports team. Sunday school, yoga class—you get the idea. You know those new neighbors a few doors down who seem so great? Here's a way to finally get to know them. Invite them to an organizational potluck for a trial dinner co-op. Or post a flier on the bulletin board at your local gourmet market, health food store, or coffee shop. Name your part of town and describe the type of foods you might like to cook. This way you can pre-qualify prospective participants so they're more likely to be a good fit.

For the ultimate recruitment tool, host a casual co-op orientation meeting of several interested parties. Get together and fill out our Compatibility Survey on page 162, and a handful of groups could be formed in a single night!

NEAR AND DEAR

Proximity is key in a neighborhood dinner co-op

One of the most important requirements of a great dinner co-op is the very close proximity of chefs to one another. The drop-off component needs to feel like a nonissue, and that's only achieved by choosing members who all live close together. Close, as in a few streets away, on the same block, or even in the same building.

No matter how great that cook may be who lives fifteen minutes away—on your night to deliver, fifteen minutes could feel like an eternity.

Remember, your own dinner is at home waiting for you to eat, too. So use the five-minute rule: by car, bike, stroller, or wagon, each chef should live no more than five minutes away from your kitchen. This rule is especially important for groups with four households rather than three.

CULINARY COMPATIBILITY

Find people who like to cook and eat

Will you embrace gourmet cuisine or simply stick with family classics made from scratch? Maybe you'll try both. As you recruit your team, have each prospective chef fill out the Compatibility Survey (see page 162). Even if you don't produce a perfect match, at least you'll know what you all do and don't have in common.

The best qualities you could find in a co-op member are open-mindedness, a willingness to try new things, and the shared love of good food. As long as everyone likes to cook and respects one another, the rest usually falls into place. Remember—it's somewhat of a transactional relationship. You don't have to sit down and eat with them every night. A friendly smile and hello is all you need as a starting point. With this in mind, use proximity and culinary compatibility as your main criteria.

If you're lucky enough to live near close friends who are great cooks, forming a co-op is easy as pie. We've found that some of the strongest, longest-running dinner co-ops were also formed by acquaintances who seemingly had little in common. Plenty of successful co-ops have wide differences in age, gender, ethnicity, and level of experience in the kitchen.

My co-op formed back when my daughter started kindergarten. I spent a few weeks just observing people. One of the things I paid attention to was how people interacted with their children—I feel that the care you put into your children is analogous to the care you put into feeding and fueling your body and family. I approached some of these parents I felt good about, and we've never looked back.

—Andy

BEST FRIENDS WHO COOK

It's a start

If you're not finding other cooks who meet the test as far as proximity and compatibility, but you're dying to try a dinner co-op, launch one with your closest friends. Consider doing a three-month trial run. That way nobody feels obligated to continue if they find a more optimal situation.

Best friends cooking together can be a dream come true—you can get some experience under your belts until you each become co-op masters. As word gets around, you may be approached individually by people who live closer or have more similar diets. Who knows, maybe your group can then split off to form two or three new co-ops that work even better to fit your lifestyles.

Know where to look
Seek out great cooks in your immediate radius

book club	Sunday school	gym
PTA meeting	golf course	poolside
soccer bleachers	bookstore	tennis court
farmers' market	office lunchroom	gourmet market
aqua aerobics	cooking class	choir practice
health food store	bunko party	bridge game
coffee shop	yoga class	park
T-ball game	neighborhood mixer	library

EXPLORE FOOD PREFERENCES

Use your veto sparingly

Before you start cooking, each household should fill out the Food Preferences worksheet on page 164 and review it together. Here is everybody's chance to veto the foods that they absolutely can't stand.

Important: challenge yourselves to veto as few items as possible. Back when you were ten, maybe it was that your mom boiled the Brussels sprouts that was such a turn off. Give your co-chefs (and the Brussels sprouts) one more chance and see what happens. Offer yourselves the widest flexibility by minimizing the number of off-limits ingredients. Otherwise, you can look forward to night after night of broiled chicken on a bed of white rice!

Once all the forms are completed, sit down together and share your preferences. Call out the ingredients like you're playing bingo, maintaining a preliminary list of no-no's. If the combined form comes back covered in red ink, it's not a winning card. If there are more than, say, 20 percent of the items circled, that's a strong hint that each household should go back and try to accept two or three ingredients they originally rejected. Once the compiled list of no-no's is manageably short, each chef goes home and posts the list for easy reference.

Go into this process knowing you could get some surprises. The Food Preferences chart can be very telling—if families have major differences, such as, "We don't eat salad," or "Nothing from the ocean," then be prepared to go back to the drawing board in terms of your overall compatibility. No hard feelings! It's better to speak up now than to be frustrated later because you can't cook the things you really love.

Kitchen Notes

Andy says: Sheila didn't check the box to say "no salmon," even though she did not like it. She decided it would be good for her children to see her be challenged with a food she didn't like. She now loves salmon and her son, Jonathan, loves it too!

Diana says: I'd always thought of myself as a broad-minded eater. Nothing was off limits . . . except cilantro. I wouldn't touch anything with cilantro in it. That all changed when Jen made her killer enchiladas laced with fresh cilantro. When she later apologized for adding the dreaded herb to her dish, I said, "What cilantro?"

Alex says: If you end up staying in a co-op for several years, you might get increasingly "macho" about what you'll eat. Some of us who started out a little picky have gradually become omnivorous thrill-seekers. I'd never go back!

That's why it's worth sharing

Was your dad a medium-rare guy or did he grill the steaks until all color was completely eradicated? What did Mom spread on sandwiches—mayo or something called "salad dressing?" Sweet pickles or dill? Wheat bread or white? From childhood, we bring a set of ingrained preferences that we're not even aware of.

It's not until you start cooking for other families that you find out where your own quirks are. Some people add olives to everything, and others won't touch an olive. You love salt, but you still think it's weird to put salt on watermelon. We advise you to observe these little quirks, appreciate them, and then let them all go. You will never meet another person who cooks (or eats) exactly the way you do. That's the joy of forming a co-op. By opening yourself to this experience, you can expose your family to foods and preparations you never would've tried in a million years. And that's a good thing.

Don't be too self-conscious about whether the group will like your style of cooking. You'll have built-in safety nets—you can put a system in place for feedback, and we recommend a trial period before you commit long-term. Keep it light, do your best, and enjoy the ride.

> At book club one night, Sarah, Liz, and I overheard someone saying "dinner co-op . . . we take turns cooking." We were all pregnant or nursing and too busy to keep up with our own appetites! The three of us made eye contact, and the deal was sealed then and there.
>
> —Alex

Kitchen Notes

Diana says: After a successful year's run, our co-op decided to branch out. We brought together fifteen interested friends for a casual co-op orientation meeting. After thirty minutes, common needs and styles were identified, and we broke out into groups. An hour later, three new co-ops were born: one was vegetarian, one was two days/week, and one was four days/week. Amazingly, all three new groups fit the five-minute rule for distance.

3

Ready, Set, Roast!

YOU'VE FOUND YOUR CIRCLE OF CHEFS—NOW IT'S TIME TO SET THE KITCHEN ON FIRE

DECIDE ON QUANTITIES

Just enough for dinner, or guaranteed leftovers?

At your first group meeting, agree on the standard number of servings you'll be delivering. There's no such thing as a "typical" family, but in our experience, co-ops often prepare four servings per family. Four servings work well not just for families of four but also for couples who enjoy packing their lunch for work the next day. Parents with babies and toddlers often do great with three servings instead of four. Singles and retirees can perhaps get by with only two servings, but it would be a shame not to have a few fabulous leftovers.

From our experience dining out, restaurant portion sizes have skewed the public's judgment of what constitutes a reasonable meal serving. Consider the USDA Center for Nutrition's rules of thumb: a portion of meat should be equivalent to a deck of cards and the starch should be about the size of a fist. We recommend a range of 4 to 6 ounces of meat per person, knowing that chops, chicken breasts, and fish fillets vary in size at the market. For vegetables, think about 3/4 to 1 cup per person or a big handful of salad greens.

The main thing is to talk about it up front and stick to the number of servings you've agreed upon. Then touch base after a month or so to evaluate how the portions are working out. Please see page 22 for our recommended containers, which will help standardize your portions and ensure that you're sending enough food for each family.

GETTING STARTED

Here are the basic to-dos before you start cooking co-operatively

1   **Recruit Chefs**
Scope out friends and neighbors. Fill out and exchange compatibility surveys. Identify your circle of chefs.

2   **Host a Kick-off Meeting**
Decide on delivery schedule and portions. Exchange contact info, review food preferences. Give and receive delivery instructions.

3   **Buy Containers**
3 families: 6 sets, each with one rectangle and one round
4 families: 10 sets, each with one rectangle and one round

Kitchen Notes

Andy says: We started off cooking three servings per family and have inched it up to four. Two families in my co-op love having leftovers, and our third family has a growing son with a bottomless pit for a stomach; so an extra serving works well for all of us.

SET YOUR WEEKLY SCHEDULE

The workweek has never been so beautiful

Have each member pick the night they'd like to cook every week. Take into account weekly meetings at work, your partner's schedule*, book club or civic meetings, kids' sports practices, etc. Then make your best guess and claim a window. The world will reorganize itself around your co-op day, and your life will be smoother than ever.

All the co-ops we've known tend to leave Friday night open to go out, order in, or just enjoy leftovers from the week. Among four-household co-ops, M-Th is common. For three-household co-ops, both M-W-Th and M-Tu-Th are popular patterns, leaving an opening mid-week.

Important: Allow yourself a minimum of two hours for preparation and delivery on your night to cook, maybe a little longer while you're still getting the hang of it.

If you have a day job, it may seem hard to clear the decks on a weekday afternoon. Think creatively! Arrange to stay fifteen minutes later every other night of the work-week if necessary. The freedom you gain is more than worth it. Mondays are popular with full-time working people who find it hard to leave the office early. Over the weekend, they prep ahead like chefs in restaurants so they need less time to cook after work.

Agree on a time for delivery and try your darnedest to never be late. We recommend a thirty-minute range, for example between 5:30 and 6:00, 6:00 and 6:30, or 6:30 and 7:00 p.m. Career people might need to deliver later and may enjoy eating a later dinner after they've had time to unwind. Families with kids are fans of early delivery—the earlier the dinner, the earlier the bedtime!

Although you'll have your standard "night to cook," it's fine to occasionally ask a group member to switch. You may have houseguests coming in or a big presentation at work, or maybe it's your anniversary. The more flexible you make your co-op, the more enjoyable it will be.

Be respectful of everyone else's calendars, and you'll be in good shape. We suggest bringing the schedule up for review every three to six months, just to make sure it's working well for everyone.

*Don't underestimate "partner power." Having a spouse or significant other on hand when you're cooking can be endlessly helpful. See page 36 for ideas on getting them involved.

Kitchen Notes

Diana says: I've been lucky in my co-ops that there's always someone else who likes to do Mondays, even though there are a lot of Monday school holidays. For me, there's nothing like coming back from a three-day weekend away to find dinner ready!

Andy says: We often change dinner delivery time during soccer season. We deliver food earlier so families can eat before practice. This is just one way we can make our co-op more convenient for everyone.

Alex says: I love my dinner co-op so much that I actually build my work schedule around my night to cook, not the other way around.

BUY YOUR CONTAINERS

Invest in a group set to make life easier

Standard dishes are not required, but they take the guesswork out of providing enough food for your group—just fill up one rectangular and one round dish per family, and you know the quantity is right.

We highly recommend a particular set of deep, straight-sided glass dishes with dark blue plastic lids. They are from Pyrex's "Storage Plus" line, a 7-cup round (1.75 quart) and an 11-cup rectangular (2.75 quart) glass container. These sizes are perfect for up to 4 to 5 servings, and they are oven-, microwave-, refrigerator-, freezer-, and dishwasher-safe. Their lids seal tightly, they stack, and they don't stain or absorb odors. These very affordable containers work beautifully for portioning and presentation of co-op dinners. They go straight from the oven, to the front porch, to the table, to the fridge. In many cases, the recipes in this book are designed to be prepared in these dishes. Find them in stores or at www.pyrexware.com.

Before Opening Week, the organizing chef can buy all the sets and each chef can pay her/his share. **A three-family co-op needs six sets of dishes and a four-family co-op needs ten sets.** Remember, a "set" is made up of one 11-cup rectangle and one 7-cup round. The dishes are owned collectively—no need to label them with names. The dishes circulate nightly, so you'll always magically have the correct number of sets on your night to cook.

Before Opening Night in a three-household co-op, the dishes should be divided up as follows: The first chef starts with three sets, second chef has two, and the last chef starts with one set. In a four-household co-op, the first chef starts with four sets, the second with three, the third with two, and the last chef starts with just one set.

Kitchen Notes

Andy says: This system is flawless as long as you don't switch cooking nights. If you do, you will need to juggle a few dishes. The dishes you need are usually just a phone call away.

Diana says: Our co-op uses additional containers and ziplock bags for salad greens, dressings, garnishes, and sauces served on the side of a meal. We don't worry about keeping track of where these inexpensive containers end up.

From the Neighborhood

I love the cycle of the Pyrex containers and the freedom they represent, sitting on our countertop waiting to be filled up.

–Chrissy on 19th Street

TUNE IN TO YOUR CIRCLE OF CHEFS

Do some menu planning—or plan NOT to plan

Even if your group is set up primarily as a transactional relationship, it always helps to know a bit about your circle of chefs. Use the first few weeks to tune in. Get to know all the family members and get a feel for their weekly routines and what they're up against.

If a chef is running late with her meal and you feel like taking a stroll, offer to pick up your dinner to save her the trip. Maybe someone's husband is always traveling—if you're home and not too busy, invite her kids to play at your house on her night to cook. These are a few simple things you can do at the beginning to build trust, goodwill, and a sense of solidarity among the chefs.

Depending on how structured you want your co-op, now may be the time to circle up for some menu planning. Start out with recipes in this book and make a meal schedule you can e-mail to the group. You'll find it's handy to know what's coming, so you'll know what not to eat for lunch.

Kitchen Notes

Andy says: We make our meal schedule in person on a calendar every six weeks or so by going out for coffee. We also make notes regarding anniversaries, birthdays, holidays, and school functions. On Sarah and Brandon's anniversary, they received a bottle of wine and a special dessert.

Alex says: Our group has never planned a thing in its life! We are as spontaneous as it gets, and every night is a true surprise. Sometimes we let the weather be our guide (cold day: Shepherd's Pie, hot day: Avocado Grapefruit Salad). Other times we buy what looks good at the market that week, or we might even shop the same day.

Think BIG for an extra boost of excitement at launch

You're embarking on a fun, potentially life-changing new project. To build excitement and momentum, set aside time together before launch to enjoy some camaraderie among the chefs. Here are some ideas to try.

Start with a Chefs Retreat: Does anyone have a cabin, condo, or perhaps a luxurious spot to pitch a tent where you all can hole up with some wine, cheese, and cookbooks? This could be an inspiring menu planning/team-building experience for your new circle of chefs. Hire someone named Sven to do the massages.

Take a Cooking Class: We'd all love to go to France or Italy for a culinary education, but until that happens, try taking a class together at your local kitchen store. It will be fun to expand your culinary boundaries together.

Plan a Field Trip to the Gourmet Store: Explore every aisle together and take turns disclosing favorite ingredients or secret tips about what goes great with what. This is also a surprisingly fun activity at the Asian or Indian market. Don't forget your purse—some ingredients you won't be able to resist.

Host Your Own Culinary Workshops: An Italian cook could demonstrate how to make fresh pasta. A wonderful baker may offer tips on baking bread or decorating a cake. The brewmaster in the group might show you how to brew your own beer—the lessons are unlimited.

Start a Cookbook Lending Library: Everyone clearly mark your cookbooks and then find an accessible shelf where you can "check out" cookbooks from one another. You'll see each other every week, so remembering to return them is easy.

Kitchen Notes

Alex says: I'll never forget the night science teacher Diana had Andy and me over to make jam with berries from the farmers market. As an alternative to the intimidating canning process, she showed us how we could use her dishwasher to get our jars hot enough to seal safely. It was the best jam I've ever tasted because we made it ourselves.

FOOD SAFETY

Agree to follow safe practices in the kitchen

Peace of mind comes from everyone being up to speed on safe food-handling practices. Nobody expects you to wear a hairnet! Your kitchen hygiene is the same as it would be for a simple family dinner—with a few twists:

1   You are now responsible for the health and happiness of more people than just your immediate family.

2   There will be some lag time between the completion of a dish and when it will be eaten by the co-op (from ten minutes to several hours).

Preventing food-borne illness

Why shouldn't you leave food out on the counter—your mother always did it? Here's what Andy learned in culinary school:

Bacteria discharge toxins that may be poisonous to humans. When you're cooking for nice people in your neighborhood, you don't want to risk food-borne illnesses caused through the growth and multiplication of bacteria. Bacteria reproduce by dividing, which means the longer food is left out in the danger zone (your counter), the more bacteria there will be.

When food rests at temperatures between 40 and 140 degrees, bacteria can survive and grow. They grow at a faster rate between 60 degrees (cool) and 120 degrees (warm). Once bacteria have grown in our food, they remain there, even after coming back to safer temperatures. When food is frozen, bacteria stop growing, but harmful bacteria are still present. Most bacteria are killed at 140 degrees, but spores will survive.

A potentially hazardous food is defined by the U.S. Public Health Service as "any food that consists in whole or in part of milk or milk products, eggs, meats, poultry, fish, shellfish, edible crustacean (shrimp, lobster, crab, etc.), baked or boiled potatoes, tofu and other soy-protein foods, plant foods that have been heat treated, raw seed sprouts, or synthetic ingredients." As a co-op chef, bear in mind that potentially hazardous foods that spend a total of more than 4 hours in the temperature danger zone have ample opportunity for bacterial contamination to take place.

You can't control how long your neighbors allow the food you delivered to stay in the danger zone before they eat. But you can keep hot foods hot and cold foods cold for as long as possible before you deliver them.

HOT-BUTTON ISSUES

Go back to the worksheets

By using our Compatibility and Food Preferences forms, you've already headed off most factors that could put a damper on your good time.

If you do find there's an issue, refer to the forms to discuss possible problems and use those words. For example, you could say, "I must be less of a [Midwestern Mama] and more of an [Asian Maven] than I thought." Or "I'm so sorry—I didn't mark off pigs feet on the form, but I realize now that I should have."

Delivery time can become a hot-button issue if you are late too often. Remember, part of the beauty of this system is the "like clockwork" aspect. Any meal, however spectacular, loses its appeal after you've eaten seventy-five crackers. Agree to a delivery time frame that you know is feasible and try like mad to be on time.

Maybe the only hot-button issues left are food quantities and what counts as an acceptable shortcut. For example, a co-op relationship might be doomed if one chef takes afternoons off to bake homemade bread for her group, only to receive Pillsbury rolls in a foil tin. The mass-produced rolls might go unnoticed in some co-ops, but it's easy to see why they wouldn't be met with enthusiasm by the artisan baker.

Have a discussion up front about approved shortcuts (bread from a bakery, prewashed salad mix, rotisserie chickens) versus those that might be collectively frowned upon (cream of mushroom soup as a base, packet sauces, or preservative-rich products ending with the word "Helper"). You might feel silly bringing it up—until you get some plastic pump cheese on your potatoes. Emphasize that what you have in mind is "from scratch" cooking and discuss what "from scratch" means to each of you. Once you have a collective vision for your co-op, hot-button issues are less likely to come up.

Kitchen Notes

Diana says: When I'm trolling for good co-op candidates, I try to explain that mega shortcuts can be a lifesaver in your everyday survival cooking, but co-op meals are different. This may sound corny, but I think of it as giving a gift to someone.

MORE FUN AT THE MARKET

A higher return on your grocery dollar

When you start your new co-op lifestyle, you will notice a change in the way you spend money for food.

The first few times you shop for co-op dinner ingredients, you may not be accustomed to spending so much on a single weeknight meal—especially if you embrace the gourmet aspect and start spending more at specialty markets pursuing organic, unusual, or expensive ingredients.

The key will be to stop shopping for all the other nights of the week. Much of what you buy will be wasted, so don't buy it. Transfer your old supermarket dollars and weeknight restaurant bills into a virtual purse you can spend at the farmers' market, butcher, baker, and gourmet store. Instant fun money! You will spend no more, and sometimes less, in the co-op model.

Here's an example for how a hundred dollars might be spent during the week to feed a family of four.

Old way

Trip to the supermarket:	$ 70.00
(includes 4 dinner ideas, each about $17.50)	
Pizza joint Friday night:	$ 30.00
	$100.00

Co-op way (shopping for one dinner)

Gourmet store/butcher:	$ 40.00
Farmers' market:	$ 20.00
Baker:	$ 10.00
Pizza joint Friday night:	$ 30.00
	$100.00

The same hundred bucks buys a heightened culinary experience with higher-quality ingredients.

Mise en place à la dinner co-op

Mise en place is a French term chefs use that means "everything in place." It means making everything as ready as it can be before you start to cook for your group.

Cookware is out, oven is preheated, vegetables are chopped, ingredients are measured. Every single thing is done, allowing you to cook without needing to stop once you get started. Without the mise en place, it would be no fun watching people cook on TV! The camera can keep rolling only because everything's been prepped in advance.

CLEAN AS YOU GO

Minimizing the mess

If cleaning the kitchen on your cooking night is up to you, that's great incentive to clean as you go. Here are a few tricks to set the stage for an easy post-meal cleanup:

» Do a quick "search and destroy" mission through your fridge before you start. You'll need extra room in there for co-op dishes before they head out for delivery.
» Evict co-op leftovers from the glass dishes. You'll need those dishes for tonight's meal. Have all the containers clean and ready.
» Start with a clean sink, empty dishwasher, and clean, clutter-free counters.
» Bring out a compost bucket or bowl and peel vegetables directly into it. Move the waste bin close to where you're working.
» Rinse and stack used pots, pans, and bowls in the sink before moving on.
» After you do the raw prep, get all the dishes out of the sink before you handle the meat. Put spices, bottles, jars, and shakers away as you finish using them.

From the Neighborhood

I am chief cheerleader, as my chef skills border on pathetic! My role is limited to salad making and cleanup after Sarah gives it her best effort to destroy the kitchen in search of the perfect meal.

–Henry on 19th Street

GET INTO THE ZONE

It's your night. Inhale, exhale. Now begin.

Enter the kitchen and clear your mind of everything that's come before this moment. Secure the perimeter. Turn off all personal electronic devices.

Begin with clean counters, an empty sink, clean kitchen towels, and a mostly empty dishwasher. Small children should be napping or playing quietly. Ha! Or maybe you can turn on PBS.*

Put on a chef's apron. Seriously, even if you've never been an apron person, buy yourself one and wear it every week on your co-op night. Why? This apron signals to the world that you mean business. It's a barrier that frees you to get messy and engage in the full-contact sport of cooking.

Bring out your recipe and illuminate the kitchen fully. As the lights come up, smile and pretend you're on TV.

*If you have older children, don't run them out of the kitchen—enlist their help. See page 48 for transforming kids into ace prep cooks.

Kitchen Notes

Andy says: Set your intentions—bring your mind to your cooking and let other things go. Put your soul into this meal.

Alex says: People understand uniforms. The apron says, "Not available to help find Polly Pocket's locket—I am poaching some lovely halibut."

Diana says: I make myself a cup of tea and read over my recipes. Then I put on my favorite music and crank it up! I may not have the best knife skills or the fanciest cookware, but on my cooking night, it's all about creating something wonderful for my friends.

4

Communication the Co-op Way

ALWAYS COMMUNICATE WITH KINDNESS TO
KEEP MORALE HIGH AND THE CUISINE INSPIRED

BE A GOOD SPORT

Attitude is everything

Being a gracious receiver—and training your family members to do the same—is an important part of keeping morale high. It goes without saying that a cheerful thank-you should greet each meal that's prepared and delivered. If your children are predisposed to nose-wrinkling on the front porch, figure out how to squelch that fast. Your dinner co-op can actually provide an amazing education for kids. (Please see page 37 for Feeding Kids and page 48 for Kids in the Kitchen.)

Weeknight cooking poses unique challenges. Along with all the dazzling meals, be prepared for inevitable hiccups. Through years of cooking in dinner co-ops, we've seen it all: salty soup, late delivery—once a glass container dropped on the street and shattered, making a nasty casserole of glass shards and sugar snap peas.

If something disastrous happens, laugh and be a good sport. Look around your clean kitchen and remember that you did not have to envision, shop for, or clean up after this meal. Put on your chef's toque and try to rescue the dinner by adding something to it from your fridge or pantry. Maybe you can dilute the extra salt or spice, mix in some rice, or put the whole thing on top of a bed of greens. In the very rare event that you can't salvage the meal, go get some takeout, order in, or treat yourselves to a fun dinner out. It's all about relaxing and being a good sport.

On the flip side, when something comes across your dinner plate that is really over the top and tickles your fancy, pick up the phone that night or the next day to give an extra thank-you.

FEEDBACK

Lots, some, or none at all

Depending on your group's style, you might want to build in a mechanism for giving and receiving feedback on your co-op dinners. Some groups routinely send e-mail feedback to the chef, while others meet socially once a month and do an informal review. Style and frequency of feedback would be a good topic to agree on at one of your early group meetings.

    Be sensitive to the lives of the people in your group. Remember, this is supposed to be fun. Everyone has an off night sometimes—if someone sort of blows it, they're usually well aware! If you're in a group that's particularly busy or overloaded with responsibility, maybe you go to a "positive only" model of feedback.

    If your group is striving toward a common goal of culinary mastery (and the members have really thick skins), it's appropriate to develop a more rigorous feedback system. That said, be nice. If you have a comment that's not a rave, make sure it's constructive. And preface it with something positive about the meal. We've found that most of the time when a dinner isn't up to par, it wasn't the cook but the recipe. Blaming the recipe can be a good neutral way to discuss shortcomings in a certain dish—in the context of "for next time."

Kitchen Notes

Andy says: Our group meets at the end of each six-week menu cycle. We declare our favorite meal from each chef and have the opportunity to ask for repeats of past meals. It's an easy way to focus on the positive.

Alex says: When we sit down, our family offers up an extra little "prayer" to the co-op chef. With a three- and five-year-old it's brief and sort of raucous: **THANK YOU [SARAH] FOR THIS GOOD SUPPER.** We encourage our kids to thank the chef personally when they love the meal.

BREAKING UP

It's not so hard to do

Co-ops need to be fun and mutually beneficial. Agree at the beginning that anyone can get out at any time for any reason. Do your part to foster an environment where people can go their own way without any hard feelings whatsoever.

Before you break up due to scheduling conflicts such as excessive busyness at work, kids, long vacations, or houseguests, consider taking a break first. Stall for a while. Believe us, the best way to learn the value of your co-op is to take a month off! (Please see Take a Break on page 40.)

If you decide to move on—no matter the reason—we recommend sticking with the classic "It's not you, it's me." We suggest at least a two- or three-week notification to allow enough time for your group to replace you. By the same token, if someone wants out, don't hassle them about it.

A great way to lay the groundwork for future reshuffling is to create a six-month "session" for your co-op. When the session ends, assume everyone will quit. Maybe everyone will sign up again, maybe they won't. If you don't renew, there should be no explanations required.

GETTING BACK TOGETHER

Pour on the charm and help out in a pinch

So you left the group but are missing it terribly. You want back in.

Begin your campaign for reentry with shameless flattery and food bribes. Reminisce about some of your favorite meals and plainly state how much you miss trading dinners. Don't expect them to read your mind and invite you back. You'll have to ask. If the group has replaced you, you've got to be respectful of that—they had every right to move on.

But don't give up yet. If it's a team of three families, maybe they can be persuaded to go up to four. If they hold firm at three or already have four, you could propose a plan in which you "share" a spot with another family. The sharing families only participate every other week, with the remainder of the co-op exchanging dinner every week.

Another successful approach is volunteering to be a guest chef whenever someone goes on vacation or needs a break. As a sub who's readily available, you may find that you give and receive more weeks than not. Or who knows, there may be a group out there who needs an experienced co-op master to get them started. You could form a whole new group that delivers the goods like never before. Good luck!

> **From the Neighborhood**
>
> Just ask! It's likely that your friends know of other people who are anxious to put a co-op of their own together. Put yourself out there with the overture that you're willing to try anything.
>
> —Jennifer on 23rd Street

Make It Fit Your Life

5

AS SOCIAL AS YOU WANT IT

Happy hour or deliver-and-dash

The primary goal of a dinner co-op is to feed three or four households with only a little more effort than it takes to feed one—and to feed them well.

You can decide how social you want your co-op to be, and your preference may change with your station in life. For example, singles and retirees might lean toward frequent group gatherings. But for mid-lifers, the dinner hour is a prized refuge of sanity after a busy day—they may prefer to escape the world and reconnect with their partner or kids over a quiet dinner at home. College students, on the other hand, may dine together several times a week, re-creating a family experience far from home. You can conduct all your co-op "business" entirely by e-mail, but a more personal connection might make it easier to communicate.

Here are a wide variety of arrangements, all of which work great:

Porch Delivery: Keep in contact through e-mail and phone calls. Leave meals in the cooler at the door. Or say hello and split.

Coffee Talk: Set a date every six weeks when the chefs can meet for coffee.

Rotating Happy Hour: Instead of making deliveries, have everyone come to your house early for a happy hour, then leave with their dinners.

Quarterly Potluck: Someone hosts a casual potluck dinner—or even easier, an after-dinner potluck dessert.

Monthly Dinner: Take turns hosting monthly dinners. Everyone comes over on your night to cook—you don't have to deliver, and families take leftovers home in Pyrex containers.

Occasional Group Picnic: Identify a nice evening and encourage everyone to meet at the same grassy spot for a picnic, "catered" by the chef whose night it is to cook.

TIME MANAGEMENT

Pressed for time? Help is all around you.

Our dream for everyone is that you can find plenty of time to savor your one night cooking. But that's not always possible, is it? There are lots of ways to save time and energy when it's your night to cook. Your dinner co-op really can be a family affair. If you have willing helpers, figure out how to use them.

Underage prep cooks

Kids can make great prep cooks. Put an apron on them and put them to work. (Please see page 49 for Age-Appropriate Kitchen Tasks.)

Spousal courier

Ask your spouse to get home early enough that one night per week to do the deliveries for you and have him/her take the kids. That way you buy yourself a few extra moments of quiet to set the table and/or celebrate your job well done with a glass of wine.

Cleanup brigade

If it's not possible for your spouse to get home in time to help prepare or deliver the meal, agree early on that he/she can be in charge of cleanup. As in: "Don't worry honey, those dishes are NOT time-sensitive!" As long as they get done eventually, right? Preferably by someone other than you.

Kitchen Notes

Diana says: My husband, Mike, is terrific about getting the kitchen ready for my night to cook—co-op dishes are staged, counters are clear, and the dishwasher is empty.

Alex says: As soon as I'm done cooking, Gary delivers the co-op dinners for me every week. Mae and Adele love to go along to see their pals Pete, Ian, and Joe. By the time they get back, my apron is off and we're ready for a nice dinner together.

If you have no helpers and are pressed for time, take shortcuts. Here are a few tricks that help:

Prewashed, precut, and precooked
It's easier than ever to find prewashed salad mix, fresh cut fruit, shredded cheeses, precooked sausages, and rotisserie chickens. These shortcuts are all fair game for your co-op cooking.

Make ahead
Some recipes require a night in the fridge. For other recipes you can prep veggies or make a dressing ahead of time. Use your crockpot to make your main meal and assemble side dishes on the fly.

Build your own
Certain sandwiches, salads, and tacos can be delivered unassembled so each diner can make a custom creation. Interactive meals are fun, and they're a snap for you to prepare and present.

FEEDING KIDS

Find out if junior likes goat cheese

With your dinner co-op, you can turn the feeding of kids from a challenge into an opportunity. Without even realizing it, sometimes we prejudice our kids against a certain food because we don't eat it ourselves. If we don't like it, we don't prepare it. If we don't prepare it, they never taste it. They go into adulthood with the dietary limitations we pass on and more than a few of their own.

Kitchen Notes

Alex says: When referring to food, our kids aren't allowed to say the words, "I don't like it." Starting as toddlers, we've asked them to say, "I don't care for any today." Maybe that sounds ridiculous from a two-year-old, but I refuse to allow them to rule out entire foods after a taste or two! So far, they will at least try most things. My philosophy is never give up—because when you do, they surely will, too. Next thing you know, you become a short-order cook.

The co-op helps. By introducing a few neutral cooks into the equation, you may discover unexpected foods that your kids take a liking to. Have fun with it—if your child loves salty foods, point out that shrimp has a salty taste. If he loves mac and cheese, give the high alert that "this pasta has cheese." Talk about something you know the child likes that this dish "reminds you of." Use some creativity and sales-manship—never assume that he won't eat the dinner. Who knows, he or she may become your family's biggest foodie.

Words from Waj

Alex and Andy's super-sharp family doctor Waj Nasser had some encouraging words about kids and dinner co-ops.

"Parents can profoundly influence a child's eating patterns as an adult, but they have to start early. Expose your kids to as broad a variety of healthy foods as are tolerable, starting as early as about six months of age.

"Parents shouldn't be afraid to have their young kids experiment with spicy, ethnic, or complex tasting 'adult' food. Guess what Thai children eat? Exactly.

"Studies suggest that even if the child rejects a certain food repeatedly, it becomes imprinted on her brain. The fact that she saw it and smelled it will make her much more likely to return to the food as an adult than if it had never been offered.

"Greater meal variety will help children achieve a healthier, balanced diet that will likely persist into adulthood. Dinner co-ops appear to be a great way parents can put kids on the right path."

–Waj Nasser, MD
Capital City Family Medicine

PICKY EATERS

How to make this fun for them

It is amazing how a dinner co-op can transform persnickety eaters. By serving them food cooked by someone else, it somehow changes the dynamic. Maybe it's the Pavlovian effect of hearing the doorbell ring. Most adults are so grateful to be receiving a meal that someone else labored over, that we try new things and enjoy many foods we never would've touched otherwise. Everything tastes better when you didn't have to make it yourself.

The goal with picky eaters in your group is to keep their palates from feeling threatened so they stay in a co-op just long enough to let go of their pickiness! You don't have to tell them that, of course. But it's true. In the spirit of trying to accommodate them (until they open up), here are a few simple things you can do.

From the Neighborhood

You can set the example—try not to be a picky eater yourself and hopefully those in your group won't be too picky, either. If there's someone in the newly forming group that has a list a mile long of things they won't eat, they might not be the right match for you.

–Jennifer on 23rd Street

Adults
Respect and adhere to the Food Preferences form. It is their life raft, and they are trusting you to not sneak things in on them. Package any spicy or "challenging" sauces or taboo food items on the side instead of mixing them in. For example, in our Roast Beef Sandwiches, put the tapenade on the side for those who don't care for olives.

Children
We've seen that the more kids are involved in cooking, the more "food adventurous" they will become. As long as the meal isn't extra spicy, urge or require kids to eat a specified amount (at least one bite). In return, allow the children of the group to help pick a "kid meal" out of a cookbook to help cook. Rotate so you end up having one specific "kid meal" every few weeks.

Kitchen Notes

Andy says: If nine-year-old Jesse is still hungry after tasting a challenging food, she may prepare something on her own, often a quesadilla, leftovers, or cereal. She must add a vegetable if she didn't eat any from the meal. As Jesse is getting older, we've seen that she likes more of the food she tries. One "kid meal" she loves to help prepare is "Giadia's Manicotti" named for her favorite chef on the Food Network.

Absence makes the heart grow fonder

Agree early on that you'll take occasional breaks from the co-op. Many people go on vacation for at least one week during the summer, and life can intervene year-round. It's a good idea to recharge and remember the difference between life with and without your dinner co-op. Here are some examples of when and how to hit the pause button:

Holidays and spring break
National holidays are a natural time to pause your co-op. During Thanksgiving week, for example, your house may be full of food already—you won't have room for more! Call off the co-op and apply yourselves to the art of home-made pie crust.

Gone fishin'
Sometimes you just need to drop off the map for a week or two. Notify your group no later than the week before and have them count you out altogether.

Vacation covered by guest chefs
If you're preparing for an extended time away, see if your group would be open to inviting a guest chef to cook and deliver in your place. After your co-op has been up and running for a while, you may find a few envious pals licking their chops to be a part of it. The results of this experiment can be fabulous—guest chefs tend to go all-out for their fifteen minutes of fame.

Kitchen Notes

Diana says: While Don and Vida were off in India for a month, we invited Chrissy to be our guest chef. It was a great experience for all of us because we were exposed to a different cooking style. Chrissy is a great cook, and when Don and Vida got back, Alex's group snatched her up for a long-term spot.

A gift to the lady with the rose bushes
Have a dinner coming to you that you don't need? Donate the incoming meal to a deserving friend or neighbor. Simply notify the lucky receiver and supply the address to your chefs (don't send them too far out of the way). Remember to retrieve the dishes and pass them on.

Free ride

Every few months, look at the calendar together and try to identify that one week in your life that's shaping up to be a monster. Ask for a free ride that week—meaning you don't cook but your family still receives—and grant the other members a free ride on the week of their choice.

Graceful cop-out

Sometimes life brings you opportunities too beautiful to refuse—like last-minute tickets to Lucinda Williams. (Co-op? What co-op?) There are many escape hatches available to you—it's all a matter of handling it gracefully. Keep reading for ideas on how to cop out in style.

Crash and burn

This is the term we use if your co-op day goes apocalyptically wrong. It's the Nuclear Option, when a graceful cop-out is no longer possible. Crash and burn means giving your group the shaft and not delivering dinner at all. Take heart, though. We are all human. Sure, your group is spoiled by delicious homemade cuisine, but way back in the back of their minds, they still remember how to make toast or operate the microwave. Crash and burn once or twice a year, and they may forgive you. More than that, and you'll be toast.

Kitchen Notes

Diana says: By two o'clock, I knew I wouldn't be able to finish making the Roasted Eggplant Lasagna I was planning for my group. The homemade sauce was done the night before, so I bailed out and used my sauce with store-bought tortellini and a veggie platter. Whew!

COPPING OUT IN STYLE

A happy ending to a bad day

In time, you will succeed in constructing an impenetrable "Don't mess with me, it's my co-op night" force field that makes you an unshakable co-op chef who cannot be blown off course by the whims of the workplace or society at large.

Until then, it's wise to admit that stuff can happen, good (a spontaneous romantic dinner) or just plain unavoidable (surprise visit from bigwigs at work) that will make it impossible to fulfill your co-op commitment in the kitchen this week. The end goal is dinner delivered on time, right? So tonight, forget the kitchen and embrace the art of copping out in style.

Restaurant delivery
Refer to your original Compatibility Surveys for ideas on your group's favorite local restaurants.. Thai and Mexican are easy alternatives. Chinese, Italian—as long as they deliver in your area, you're good to go.

Pizza
Pizza is always a good option and universally popular with kids. Include a nice salad and order toppings the families like. It's a great idea to have a standing pizza order on file (see page 168 for the Co-Op Member Profile). If you don't know what everyone likes, take a minute to call and ask. You may be copping out, but at least they can't say you're insensitive!

Grab and go
In recent years, gourmet markets have beefed up their "grab and go" cases to include some pretty exotic prepared entrées and even freshly made sushi. You may be able to score the dinners at the store and deliver directly to your co-op members without heading home. Sweeten the deal with gourmet cookies, sparkling lemonade, or a big bottle of imported beer.

Kebabs on the grill
If you have a little more time, check out your supermarket's meat and seafood counters. You may find some nice pre-stuffed or marinating foods that you can finish at home. If you have a gas grill, buy marinated, pre-threaded kebabs that grill in no time. Add rice or a simple salad and you're ready.

Kitchen Notes

Andy says: Everybody got pizza the day Jesse broke her arm.

HERO CHEFS IN THE NEIGHBORHOOD

Offering support has never been easier

One unexpected aspect of your dinner co-op is that it's like a built-in emergency response system for your life. From the beginning of time, what have people always done when someone dies, falls ill, or gives birth to a baby? You guessed it. We drop off food.

Being a member of a co-op, you position yourself as a superstar emergency responder. You are practiced at preparing and delivering large quantities of food—good food that people want and need. Since you're cooking for your group anyway, it's easy to prepare a few extra portions now and then for friends or acquaintances who are ill, grieving, or overwhelmed. And if your own family suffers a setback, just tap in to the network and you've got instant nutritional support—maybe even for weeks.

What Words Can't Express, Dinners Can

When our friend Michele's dear dad Anthony died, she had to fly thousands of miles across the country for the funeral. While she was away, e-mails were zipping back and forth through her support network, many of whom belong to dinner co-ops. By the time she got home, she received a coordinated plan for nearly four weeks of support that helped Michele and her sons get through a very tough time.

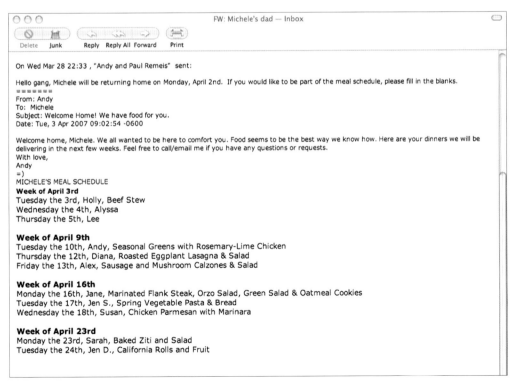

FW: Michele's dad — Inbox

Delete　Junk　　Reply　Reply All　Forward　　Print

On Wed Mar 28 22:33 , "Andy and Paul Remeis" sent:

Hello gang, Michele will be returning home on Monday, April 2nd. If you would like to be part of the meal schedule, please fill in the blanks.
=======
From: Andy
To: Michele
Subject: Welcome Home! We have food for you.
Date: Tue, 3 Apr 2007 09:02:54 -0600

Welcome home, Michele. We all wanted to be here to comfort you. Food seems to be the best way we know how. Here are your dinners we will be delivering in the next few weeks. Feel free to call/email me if you have any questions or requests.
With love,
Andy
=)
MICHELE'S MEAL SCHEDULE
Week of April 3rd
Tuesday the 3rd, Holly, Beef Stew
Wednesday the 4th, Alyssa
Thursday the 5th, Lee

Week of April 9th
Tuesday the 10th, Andy, Seasonal Greens with Rosemary-Lime Chicken
Thursday the 12th, Diana, Roasted Eggplant Lasagna & Salad
Friday the 13th, Alex, Sausage and Mushroom Calzones & Salad

Week of April 16th
Monday the 16th, Jane, Marinated Flank Steak, Orzo Salad, Green Salad & Oatmeal Cookies
Tuesday the 17th, Jen S., Spring Vegetable Pasta & Bread
Wednesday the 18th, Susan, Chicken Parmesan with Marinara

Week of April 23rd
Monday the 23rd, Sarah, Baked Ziti and Salad
Tuesday the 24th, Jen D., California Rolls and Fruit

6 | Co-Op as an Art Form

YOU'RE AN EXPERIENCED COOK—NOW PREPARE
TO BECOME A DINNER CO-OP MASTER CHEF

CULINARY SCHOOL IN YOUR OWN KITCHEN

A subtle transformation from cook to chef

After you've cooked in a co-op for a year or so, you may be surprised at how far you've come. A transformation has been underway—by now you've gained nearly unshakable confidence in the kitchen.

Through this year-round system, you've bought yourself the time to take on more challenging recipes and to experiment with new ingredients and presentations. Your knife skills are better. You've learned to improvise, to recover, and to present with a smile.

Regular co-op cooking can elevate your game for weekend entertaining, too. Suddenly the idea of hosting a dinner party doesn't faze you in the least. In some ways it's easier—you cook the same quantity you're used to but don't need to deliver. When a co-op chef has people over, she's not faking it! Everything really is under control.

Once you've got months of "fulfilling the commitment" under your belt, we challenge you to take your co-op cooking to the next level. Tap in to your full spectrum of creativity and test your limits as a chef.

> From the Neighborhood
>
> I have learned so much from cooking for twelve every week. I learned to organize better, to use my cooking tools, and to improve my skills. Best of all, my confidence level has gone way up. A dinner party for six seems like a breeze now.
>
> –Vida on Berkeley Street

MAKE FRIENDS WITH THE SAUSAGE LADY

Ingredients are half the fun

You're no longer a shopper, you're a chef. And chefs don't shop, they procure. Now that you're only preparing one special dinner a week, allow yourself some freedom from the metal shopping cart. When possible, try buying ingredients not from stores, but from *people*.

In today's global food market, the exotic end product seems to lose something. Of course everything looks beautiful, but it somehow lacks context and value. What should feel like a miracle has become a commodity. We're told that our produce travels an average of 1,500 miles from farm to plate, a troubling distance considering the skilled farmers and ranchers in our own communities.

When you can look into the person's eyes who produced your food, it's priceless. Just think, if a woman drove her truck fifty miles to set up a card table, cooler, and hot samples (in the rain), she must believe there's something special about her sausage. And she's probably right.

Jump in to your new role as a chef and make friends with the sausage lady. Grow your own heirloom tomatoes and herbs. Brag to your co-op about where you got the corn for their chowder. Go ahead, give them the time the fish left the sea. They will eat it up—literally.

Kitchen Notes

Alex says: I was at our local gourmet store when I met a tall, stoic old man silently handing out samples of these fantastic dried apples. The packaging said "Uncle Lou's Dried Apples." Gulping down my second one, I peered into his face and asked, "Are you Lou?" When he said yes, I bought as many as I could afford.

Buy local and eat what's in season

Local ingredients are hot items on today's restaurant menus. Chefs procure local ingredients in season for their superior flavor and texture. There are endless benefits—health, social, and environmental—to buying your food locally. To find local producers of sustainably farmed foods for use in your own dinner co-op, go to **www.sustainabletable.org** and just type in your zip code.

Across the U.S. and Canada, adventurous "locavores" are signing on to the 100-Mile Diet, striving to only consume food grown within a specified radius. Could be a life-changing experiment to try with your dinner co-op: **www.100milediet.org.**

GROW YOUR OWN ANYTHING

Your backyard is as "local" as food can get

It doesn't matter if you're snipping herbs from a pot outside the kitchen door or harvesting bushels of tomatoes to make your own salsa—the feeling is the same.

It's hugely satisfying to grow something—anything—and prepare it for your family and friends to eat. Your co-op will cherish those freshest of ingredients, and you'll have the thrill of harvesting and eating food still warm from the sun. The most celebrated chefs have turned to kitchen gardens to supplement or full-on supply their restaurants for good reason—foods in season and "just plucked" are amazingly fresh and taste wonderful.

We grow our own for lots of reasons:

» **It's cheaper.** We get fresh herbs and organic produce practically for free!
» **It's fresher.** It hasn't been in anybody's car, truck, or train.
» **It's better tasting.** Store-bought tomatoes are just not the same as vine-ripened.
» **It's educational.** How else do kids learn where those sugar snap peas come from?
» **It's exciting.** From seed, to plant, to bean, to dinner! It all happens right there in front of you.

> **From the Neighborhood**
>
> We have several portions of our dinners homegrown in people's gardens—fresh vegetables, herbs, and fruits. It's delicious, fresh, and helps us share with our kids that you can indeed grow your own food and not just buy it at the store.
>
> **–Janet on Parkside**

Have some sunny space that already gets hit by the sprinkler? Try these:

arugula	pumpkins
basil	sugar snap peas
chives	thyme
lettuce	tomatoes
parsley	watermelon

Even if you're not the green thumb type, you could throw some starter plants in a pot by the back door and see what happens. If nothing happens, you haven't lost much. But if you get to do some snipping and call it dinner, you've gotten more than you gave. And it just might grow on you.

KIDS IN THE KITCHEN

Eager gardeners and prep cooks are right under your nose

Once you're in the swing of your co-op and have everything under control, consider bringing your kids on board as serious helpers. Our kids have started as prep cooks and the oldest is approaching sous chef status! Patience is a virtue—be sure to start with small expectations when they're younger and gradually give them more to do. You may find yourself looking forward to your cooking day for a much different reason than when you started.

Kitchen Notes

Andy says: Jesse and I really have a fun time in the kitchen. Over the years, she has learned to do more and more without as much guidance. It is great to see her confidence grow. Cooking co-op meals with my daughter has taught her many great life skills: how to cook, how to work together, and the value of helping others.

Junior High Garden Club
Too cool for school

Diana started a vegetable gardening club at the junior high where she teaches. Teenagers grow whatever strikes their fancy and then munch away right out of the garden. Many of the kids had no idea how big a vine it takes to grow a watermelon or what spinach looks like in the ground. They learn very quickly that homegrown veggies and fruits taste fantastic—and who could resist after fussing over them for weeks? Kevin, 13, didn't like tomatoes until he popped a sweet yellow pear tomato that he grew himself into his mouth. He said, "These taste different than tomatoes I've had before."

Teenagers who aren't afraid to get their hands dirty—in our book, it doesn't get much cooler.

Age-appropriate kitchen tasks

5 years and under
pick herbs
stem cilantro
scrub potatoes
wipe mushrooms
shuck corn
sprinkle cheese
stem fresh thyme and rosemary
paint garlic butter onto bread
sort out bruised berries
work the salad spinner
run the blender with help
taste everything
make butter*

6–9 years
All of the above, plus:
measure ingredients
run the blender
help choose recipes
knead dough
stir continuously
crack eggs
wash fruits/vegetables
thread skewers
whisk vigorously
crank pasta machine
assemble salads
layer lasagnas
package up extras
set the table

10–12 years
All of the above, plus:
toast nuts
mash potatoes
grate cheese
begin learning knife skills
make croutons
deliver a meal, if close by

13–18 years
All of the above, plus:
dice onion
mince garlic
make vinaigrette
wash pots and pans
set the table
pour the chef more wine
work toward making the whole
   co-op dinner once monthly

*Homemade butter
To keep little ones busy while you cook, fill a jar halfway with heavy cream. Tightly screw on the lid and start shaking the jar. After less than fifteen minutes of shaking, you'll have real homemade butter! Stop shaking when a ball forms in the jar. Pour off the excess liquid, add a little salt, then refrigerate to firm up the butter. Add fresh herbs or garlic and serve to your co-op with fresh-baked bread.

Kitchen Notes

Alex says: I get such a kick out of sending my three-year-old into the herb garden for four snips of parsley. Our in-town yard isn't quite big enough for a vegetable garden, but Adele knows all her herbs and loves the honor of collecting them for dinner.

FRILLS AND CHILLS: MAKE IT FESTIVE

Weeknight dinners can be beautiful

Use your co-op as an outlet for creativity. If you've mastered the basics and have creativity to spare, surprise your group and spoil them with festive and unexpected presentations. Whether it's a special occasion or a regular Tuesday night, it doesn't take much to impress weary desk-jockeys after a hard day at the office.

Supplies
doilies
frilly toothpicks
decorative dish towels
colored florists' foils
brown bags with handles
decorative cello bags
kitchen twine
parchment paper
raffia
baskets
antique picnic hampers

cut flowers from radishes and carrots
cinnamon sticks
cut fans of pear, apple, or strawberry

Ideas
details of exciting ingredients
"monogrammed" foods
secret messages
personalized fortunes
horoscopes
hidden treasures
handmade greeting cards

Garnishes
fresh berries
herb blossoms
pickled peppers
curly kale
scored cucumbers

Extras
after-dinner truffles
hand-dipped strawberries
(See Quick Sides and Extras, page 152
   for more ideas)

Fresh Herbs and Flowers

Tie bundles of fresh herbs, such as rosemary, blooming chives, oregano, or sage. Bake fresh lavender in with your shortbread cookies.

Use edible fresh flowers (no pesticides) to garnish dishes or to adorn a salad. Try nasturtiums, pansies, rose petals, violas, calendulas, chrysanthemums, honeysuckle, impatiens, lavender, jasmine, and primrose.

Kitchen Notes

Alex says: For most people, "homemade" is a major upgrade all by itself. Nobody ever **expects** you to take it to this level. These ideas are for when you're really feeling it.

MOOD FOOD

Now you have an audience for this stuff

From the Neighborhood

I got a kick out of delivering Chrissy's ratatouille the same night the movie came out in theaters.

–Rich on 19th Street

Since you'll be seeing your co-op members every week, you'll gain a pretty good idea of what's going on in their lives. Tune in to the collective mood and use the weather, holidays, or pop-culture favorites to inspire your cooking. Here are some examples of special thematic dinners you could deliver to the group. Use your imagination and present your own mood food—when it strikes you.

Films, Books, and Pop Culture
Babette's Feast
Green Eggs and Ham
Big Night
French Laundry
Mystic Pizza
Like Water for Chocolate
Napoleon Dynamite
Iron Chef

Cultural
Olympic Games Opening Ceremony
Thai One On
Fat Tuesday (Mardi Gras)
French Pique-Nique
Chinese New Year
Indian Wedding
Luck of the Irish
Cinco de Mayo
Passover Traditions
Legal for Lent

Seasonal
Fall Harvest
Back to School Pot Roast Dinner
Tailgating the Big Game
Oktoberfest
First Day of Summer
Tastes of Spring
Winter Whiteout

Tributes
Birthday Dinner with Cupcakes
Schoolkids' Honor Roll Bonus Night
We Are the Champions

Romantic
Dinner and a Movie
1950s Honeymoon in Hawaii
Happy Anniversary, Baby
Vampish Valentines Dinner with
   Candles

Kitchen Notes

Alex says: One weeknight when we all had toddlers, Liz delivered homemade waffles in the shape of cows, horses, and barns, along with the finest maple syrup and link sausages. The kids went wild, and the adults ate it up, too.

CHANGING YOUR LIFESTYLE?

Evolve your co-op

If your dietary needs change, try to bring your group along for the journey. Before simply withdrawing, go public with your situation—other members might be facing similar issues, too. When modifying your diet, your co-op can become the ultimate support group. And as a team, you can reach your goals much more easily.

We've seen groups agree to accommodate a wide range of needs among members. Here are some examples of dramatic dietary changes that are within your reach with co-operative cooking.

Weight loss

Watching cholesterol

Nutrition for pregnancy

Becoming vegetarian

Craving more meat

Incorporating more fish

Athletic training

Going local/100-Mile Diet

Nutrition for nursing

Need more fiber

Managing diabetes

Going dairy-free

Going all organic

Low sodium/hypertension

Where will you take YOUR dinner co-op? May you live long, eat well, and enjoy a new sense of balance at dinner time.

Diana   Alex   Andy :)

An ideal co-op dinner has great flavor, travels well, is balanced and nutritious, presents beautifully, and tastes just as good the next day.

Not every good recipe will work for your dinner co-op. Meats, for example, tend to dry out if they're not eaten right away, making them trickier to use in co-op meals. Our recipes include sauces and moist preparations to solve this problem.

The recipes we present are designed to help shake up your average weeknight dinner. Our recipes feed twelve but can be adjusted for any size dinner co-op. Have fun putting together innovative combinations and seeking fresh, seasonal, and local ingredients to share. Put your soul into the recipe—we guarantee everything will taste better.

Our philosophy on cooking

We've honed our style from a wide variety of sources. Certain four-star chefs have influenced us greatly—Thomas Keller, Alice Waters, Rick Bayless, Molly Katzen, and Deborah Madison—maybe you'll catch glimpses of these great talents in our recipes. We've treasured their cookbooks and now aim to bring our own brand of four-star home cooking to the neighborhood. As a test kitchen, Molly Katzen had the famous Moosewood Restaurant and Thomas Keller had the French Laundry. Our test kitchen was the neighborhood—a network of good cooks fired up their home kitchens to put these recipes to the test.

In the process, we learned that our real heroes are alive and well, right down the street. They're the kitchen staff, the wait staff, and management all in one. Our hero chefs enter the kitchen after a big day at work, chasing kids, or changing the world. They pour their own wine, roll up their sleeves, and go for it.

RECIPES

Salads

Soups

Meats

Fish and Seafood

Poultry

Recipes continued on next page.

Vegetarian Main Dishes

Sandwiches and Pizzas

Sandwiches

Pizzas

Vegetables

Spring and Summer

Fall and Winter

Grains and Rice

Avocado and Grapefruit Salad with Chile Maple Pecans

SERVES 12

THE TART GRAPEFRUIT, CREAMY AVOCADO, AND SALTY/SWEET NUTS ARE TERRIFIC COMPLEMENTS IN THIS ELEGANT, FRESH-TASTING SALAD. THE CHILE MAPLE PECANS ARE A TREAT YOU CAN ROAST A DAY AHEAD. CONSIDER MAKING EXTRAS—THEY'RE SO GOOD YOU'LL WANT TO SNACK ON THEM LATER. BUTTER LETTUCE WORKS ESPECIALLY WELL WITH THIS COMBINATION OF FLAVORS.

CHILE MAPLE PECANS

2	CUPS PECAN HALVES
½	CUP MAPLE SYRUP
2	TABLESPOONS ANCHO CHILE POWDER*
½	TEASPOON SALT
3	TABLESPOONS SUGAR

SALAD

2	HEADS BUTTER LETTUCE, TORN
2	AVOCADOES, SLICED
3	PINK GRAPEFRUIT, SECTIONED**
1	RED ONION, THINLY SLICED

LIME VINAIGRETTE

½	CUP FRESH LIME JUICE*
1	TEASPOON SALT
1	TEASPOON SUGAR
1	CUP OLIVE OIL
	PEPPER TO TASTE

DRESSING

(PACKAGE SEPARATELY)

PREPARED ITALIAN VINAIGRETTE (NEWMAN'S OWN OR BERNSTEIN'S RESTAURANT ARE GOOD CHOICES)

OR LIME VINAIGRETTE

CHILE MAPLE PECANS Preheat oven to 350 degrees F.

Stir together pecans and maple syrup in a bowl. Spread out on a shallow sheet pan. Combine chile powder, salt, and sugar. Sprinkle chile mixture over the nuts and bake 10 minutes, until toasted. Stir twice during baking. Remove nuts to parchment paper to cool, separating them so they don't stick together.

SALAD Divide lettuce among serving containers (about a handful of lettuce for each person) and arrange remaining ingredients on top. Garnish with Chile Maple Pecans.

LIME VINAIGRETTE Place lime juice, salt, and sugar in a blender and slowly add olive oil in a thin stream while blending. This will emulsify the oil and juice. Add pepper to taste. Divide dressing among small serving containers for each family.

*See Special Ingredients for the Co-op Cook on page 155.

**Use a sharp paring knife to remove skin and white pith from each grapefruit. Then pop the segments out cleanly by slipping the knife between each segment and membrane.

Pesto Chickpeas and Mixed Greens

SERVES 12

HERE'S AN EASY, INVENTIVE ALTERNATIVE TO A HO-HUM GREEN SALAD. OUR VEGETARIAN
CO-OP FRIENDS LIKE THE ADDITION OF CHICKPEAS TO BOOST THE PROTEIN IN A MEATLESS MEAL.

PESTO DRESSING

- 1½ CUPS FRESH BASIL LEAVES, PACKED
- ⅔ CUP FRESH LEMON JUICE
- 1¼ CUPS OLIVE OIL
- ½ CUP PARMESAN, GRATED
  SALT AND PEPPER TO TASTE

SALAD

- 28 OUNCES CANNED CHICKPEAS (GARBANZO BEANS), DRAINED AND RINSED
- 4 MEDIUM TOMATOES, CUT INTO THIN WEDGES
- 1 HANDFUL SALAD GREENS PER PERSON

GARNISH SUGGESTION
(PACKAGE SEPARATELY)

PINE NUTS, TOASTED

PESTO DRESSING Put basil and lemon juice in a food processor and blend until smooth. Slowly add olive oil while processing. Transfer dressing to a medium bowl. Stir in cheese, and salt and pepper to taste.

SALAD Add chickpeas to dressing and toss to coat. Divide the chickpeas equally between the serving dishes. Place tomato wedges on top of chickpeas in serving dish.

Wash, tear, and divide salad greens into separate plastic bags for each household. To serve, put greens on plate and spoon salad on top.

> The texture of the chickpeas together with the flavor of fresh basil is fabulous.
>
> –Jennifer on 23rd Street

Asian Noodle Slaw

SERVES 12

THIS IS LIKE A WILD PARTY IN YOUR MOUTH. PURPLE CABBAGE AND NOODLES COMBINE TO MAKE A CRUNCHY, COLORFUL SALAD TO CHASE AWAY WEEKNIGHT BOREDOM. LIME, SESAME OIL, AND GINGERROOT KEEP IT LIGHT AND TANGY. IF YOUR GROUP LIKES IT SPICY, USE MORE CHILI OIL. WHEN SERVING AS A MAIN DISH, INCREASE THE AMOUNT BY HALF AND CONSIDER TOPPING WITH SHRIMP OR CHICKEN.

DRESSING

4	TABLESPOONS RICE WINE VINEGAR
2	TABLESPOONS SESAME OIL
1/3	CUP FRESH LIME JUICE (ZEST LIMES FIRST AND RESERVE ZEST, SEE BELOW)
2/3	CUP OLIVE OIL
2	TABLESPOONS FRESH GINGER, MINCED
2	TABLESPOONS SOY SAUCE
1	TABLESPOON HONEY
3	TABLESPOONS SMOOTH PEANUT BUTTER
	DASH CHILI OIL

SALAD

4	small packages RAMEN NOODLES (TRY WHOLE-WHEAT FOR MORE FLAVOR)
4	CUPS SUGAR SNAP PEAS, TRIMMED
1/2	MEDIUM HEAD PURPLE CABBAGE, SHREDDED*
1	CUP DAIKON RADISH CURLS (MADE WITH VEGETABLE PEELER)
2/3	CUP CILANTRO, CHOPPED
1	CUP RED BELL PEPPER, JULIENNED
6	GREEN ONIONS, SLICED
2	LIMES, ZESTED

GARNISH SUGGESTION

ROASTED PEANUTS, CRUSHED**

DRESSING Combine ingredients in a blender and whirl until smooth.

SALAD Cook noodles in boiling water. Place snap peas in a strainer and pour noodles and water over them. This will give snap peas a brief period in hot water. (Alternately, blanch snap peas separately for 20 seconds.) Allow noodles and snap peas to cool. Combine remaining ingredients in a large bowl with noodles and snap peas. Add dressing and toss.

*Shredding Cabbage: Cut in quarters and core. Working with a quarter section at a time, rest a cut side of the cabbage down on your cutting board and slice very thinly, starting at one end. You will be amazed at how quickly this goes.

**Crushing Peanuts: There are three ways to do this. 1) Use the flat side of a knife to smash the nuts on a cutting board, 2) Place them in a ziplock bag and use a rolling pin or meat tenderizer, or 3) Just chop with a knife.

Serve Broiled Tuna with Miso, Lime, and Ginger Sauce (see page 96) alongside this salad—great complementary flavors! For a change of taste and color, substitute savoy cabbage for the purple cabbage.

Mexican Salad with Corn, Mango, and Tomatoes

SERVES 12

ENJOY THE RAINBOW OF COLORS AND FRESH TASTES IN THIS PERENNIAL FAVORITE. THOUGH IT WORKS GREAT ALONGSIDE MEXICAN ENTRÉES, IT GOES WELL WITH MOST ANYTHING AND IS A STAND-ALONE HIT AT POTLUCKS AND BOOK CLUB MEETINGS.

3	MANGOES, PEELED AND DICED
2	PINTS CHERRY TOMATOES, HALVED
½	RED ONION, THINLY SLICED
6	EARS FRESH CORN*
½	CUP CHOPPED CILANTRO
½	CUP FRESH LIME JUICE**
	SALT AND PEPPER TO TASTE
1	HANDFUL SALAD GREENS PER PERSON

GARNISH SUGGESTION

12   OUNCES FETA, CRUMBLED

Gently toss together ingredients from mangoes through lime juice, salt and pepper to taste, and then divide into co-op containers.

Wash, tear, and divide salad greens into separate plastic bags for each household. To serve, put greens on plate and spoon salad on top.

*Corn: Cut fresh kernels off the cob or substitute 1 cup frozen corn for each ear.

**See Special Ingredients for the Co-op Cook on page 155.

> This salad is a bright summer's day in a bowl.
>
> –Sarah on 16th Street

Antipasto Panzanella Salad

SERVES 12

THIS HEARTY SALAD UPGRADES ITALIAN ANTIPASTO FROM AN APPETIZER TO A COMPLETE ENTREE. BITS OF BREAD MIXED WITH SALAMI, PEPPERS, ARTICHOKE HEARTS, AND OLIVES GET A PEPPERY KICK FROM AN EASY BALSAMIC VINAIGRETTE. TO MAKE IT A LITTLE HEARTIER, TOSS IN CUBED MOZZARELLA AND SERVE ON A SMALL BED OF MIXED GREENS. THIS DISH TASTES SURPRISINGLY GOOD ON DAY TWO AS LEFTOVERS.

22 OUNCES CANNED CANNELLINI BEANS (WHITE KIDNEY), RINSED AND DRAINED

28 OUNCES ARTICHOKE HEARTS, DRAINED AND QUARTERED

3 ROASTED RED BELL PEPPERS, FROM A JAR OR HOMEMADE, DICED

1½ CUPS KALAMATA OLIVES OR GREEN OLIVES, STUFFED WITH BLUE CHEESE

1½ CUPS PEPPERONCINI, DRAINED (ABOUT 24)

¾ SMALL RED ONION, SLICED

2 OUNCES FRESH BASIL LEAVES, ROUGHLY CHOPPED

3 TABLESPOON CAPERS, RINSED AND DRAINED

½ CUP OLIVE OIL

½ CUP BALSAMIC VINEGAR
SALT AND PEPPER TO TASTE

1 LOAF DAY-OLD* BREAD FROM YOUR FAVORITE ARTISAN, CUBED

6 ROMA TOMATOES, QUARTERED

SALAD TOPPINGS

1 POUND SALAMI, THINLY SLICED

6 HARD-BOILED EGGS (OPTIONAL), PEELED AND QUARTERED

6 OUNCES PARMESAN, SHAVED

In a large bowl, combine ingredients from cannellini beans through capers.

In a second bowl, mix olive oil and vinegar together with a little salt and pepper. Add bread and mix. Fold in tomatoes; combine with ingredients from large bowl and portion into co-op dishes.

Individually roll up sliced salami and stick rolls decoratively along edges of co-op dish. Place egg quarters gently at ends and pile Parmesan in the middle. You're ready to go.

*Day-old Bread: As good bread starts to get hard, just cube the remaining and put it in the freezer in ziplock bags. When you have acquired enough bread, it is time to make this recipe. You may also use fresh bread. Cube it and then bake on cookie sheet at 250 degrees F until dried out.

> This salad has a wonderful mix of color from the tomatoes, roasted red peppers, basil, and pepperoncinis. With the salami, Parmesan, and chilled hard-boiled eggs, it makes a perfect warm-weather dinner.
>
> –Kim on Cherokee Place

This dish pairs nicely with our Roasted Asparagus Soup with Lemon (see page 76) or serve it on its own with a fruit side or dessert.

Tangy Spinach Salad with Dried Pears and Blue Cheese

SERVES 12

SWEET AND SALTY, CREAMY YET CRUNCHY—THIS SALAD HAS IT ALL. THE TANGY DRESSING TIES ALL OF THESE FLAVORS TOGETHER IN A SUMPTUOUS SALAD PERFECT AS A SIDE OR A LIGHT ENTRÉE. THE DISTINCTIVE ZESTY DRESSING ALSO DOUBLES AS A MARINADE FOR PORK TENDERLOIN, TOFU, OR FLANK STEAK. GRILL OR SAUTÉ YOUR FAVORITE PROTEIN AND SERVE IT NESTLED ON THE SALAD TO MAKE A MAIN COURSE.

DRESSING

⅓ CUP RED WINE VINEGAR
⅓ CUP DRY RED WINE
⅓ CUP HONEY
¼ CUP SUGAR
1 CUP KETCHUP
1 TABLESPOON WORCESTERSHIRE SAUCE
2 TEASPOONS DIJON MUSTARD
2 TEASPOONS CURRY POWDER
2 TEASPOONS DRIED DILL WEED
4 CLOVES GARLIC, MINCED
1 CUP OLIVE OIL

SALAD

16 OUNCES FRESH SPINACH LEAVES, LARGE STEMS REMOVED
1 OUNCE BASIL, CHIFFONADE*
6 BABY WHITE TURNIPS, SLICED (SUBSTITUTE RADISHES IF NEEDED)
1 CUP COARSELY CHOPPED DRIED PEARS**
¾ CUP SLICED ALMONDS, TOASTED
12 OUNCES BLUE CHEESE, CRUMBLED

DRESSING Whisk together everything in a large bowl. Package dressing in separate containers for each family. Set aside at room temperature for 30 minutes or up to 2 hours to blend flavors. Dressing will keep for up to 2 weeks in the refrigerator.

SALAD Toss spinach and basil together. Divide among serving dishes.

Arrange turnips and pears on top of greens. Sprinkle almonds and cheese on last. As an option, you can package up the nuts and cheese in small bags so that each person can add what they want after the salad is dressed.

*Chiffonade is a French term that means thin strips or shreds of raw vegetables, often used for a garnish. To easily chiffonade basil, stack the leaves on top of each other, placing a large one on the bottom. Starting from the tip, roll the stack up. Hold the rolled basil and cut small slices off the edges until your whole stack is in cool julienne strips.

**When in season, fresh pears can be used to add a twist in texture, color, and flavor.

> **My kids love this spinach salad!**
>
> –Holly on Skylark Drive

We like this dressing so much we use it in our recipe for Tofu Triangles with Caramelized Onions and Smoked Paprika Red Peppers (see page 118).

Caesar Salad with Shaved Parmesan and Zesty Blender Dressing

SERVES 12

EVERYONE HAS A FAVORITE CAESAR SALAD RECIPE—THIS IS OURS. THE INCLUSION OF BUTTERMILK GIVES IT A RICH COMPLEXITY, AND THE AUTHENTIC CAESAR FLAVOR COMES FROM THE GENEROUS USE OF ANCHOVIES. NOT TO WORRY—THE ANCHOVIES ARE THOROUGHLY BLENDED, AND EVEN THOSE WHO CLAIM AN AVERSION TO ANCHOVIES LOVE THIS NICELY BALANCED DRESSING.

DRESSING

6	CLOVES GARLIC, CHOPPED
1	SHALLOT, CHOPPED
2–4	OUNCES ANCHOVIES, IN OLIVE OIL (NOT DRAINED)
2	LEMONS, JUICED
2	TABLESPOONS DIJON MUSTARD
2	TABLESPOONS WORCESTERSHIRE SAUCE
½	CUP BUTTERMILK
½	CUP MAYONNAISE
½	TEASPOON SUGAR
½	CUP OLIVE OIL
	SALT AND PEPPER TO TASTE

SALAD

3	HEADS ROMAINE, CHOPPED
3	CUPS CROUTONS*

GARNISH SUGGESTION

6	OUNCES PARMESAN, SHAVED**

DRESSING Combine everything but oil, salt, and pepper in a blender and whirl until smooth. With blender running, drizzle oil into dressing until desired consistency is attained. Salt and pepper to taste. Divide the dressing equally among serving containers and refrigerate if dressing is to sit longer than one hour. Makes 2 ½ cups.

SALAD Divide lettuce and croutons into separate serving containers and refrigerate romaine.

GARNISH SUGGESTION Divide shaved cheese among separate serving containers and refrigerate.

*Croutons: Freeze day-old bread in an airtight container to make homemade croutons any time.

**Shaving Parmesan into longer paper-thin sheets contributes to a beautiful presentation. To shave Parmesan or other hard cheese, use a vegetable peeler.

Serve with grilled shrimp, Salmon with Fresh Strawberry Relish (see page 99), or Rosemary Lime Chicken (see page 106).

CROUTONS

4	CUPS CUBED BREAD (IT'S FUN TO USE A VARIETY OF GOOD-QUALITY BREADS)
3	TABLESPOONS OLIVE OIL
	SALT TO TASTE

BACON AND AVOCADO VARIATION

12	OUNCES BACON, COOKED AND CRUMBLED
3	GREEN ONIONS, THINLY SLICED
2	AVOCADOES, DICED
28	OUNCES QUARTERED ARTICHOKE HEARTS, DRAINED

CROUTONS Preheat oven to 350 degrees F.

Mix ingredients together and spread out on a sheet pan. Bake for 15 minutes, stirring occasionally. Cool and store in an airtight container.

BACON AND AVOCADO VARIATION Follow the directions for Caesar Salad and package these additional ingredients with the Romaine.

> A great recipe that has become my kitchen standard!
>
> –Kristy on Whidden Street

Ginger Apple Coleslaw

SERVES 12

ANDY'S FRIEND ELISABETH CALLED ONE NIGHT TO SAY SHE REALLY LIKED THE DINNER AND LOVED THE APPLE IN THE COLESLAW. IT'S GREAT TO HEAR A SIX-YEAR-OLD SO ENTHUSIASTIC ABOUT CABBAGE! WHEN YOU MAKE THIS SALAD AHEAD OF TIME, CUT THE APPLES LAST. THE DRESSING AND THE VEGETABLES MAY BE KEPT IN THE REFRIGERATOR SEPARATELY. AS DINNERTIME APPROACHES, JUST TOSS EVERYTHING TOGETHER AND YOU'RE READY.

DRESSING

1	CUP PLAIN YOGURT
1	CUP MAYONNAISE
⅓	CUP RICE VINEGAR
¼	CUP OLIVE OIL
¼	CUP FRESH LIME JUICE*
¼	CUP MINCED FRESH GINGER*

SALAD

1	HEAD SAVOY OR GREEN CABBAGE, SHREDDED**
½	HEAD PURPLE CABBAGE, SHREDDED**
4	CARROTS, PEELED AND JULIENNED (OR BUY IN BAG "SHREDDED")
½	LARGE DAIKON RADISH,*** PEELED AND DICED
¾	CUP DRIED MANGO, LIGHTLY SWEETENED, DICED SMALL
2	GRANNY SMITH APPLES, DICED

GARNISH SUGGESTIONS

CILANTRO OR FRESH MINT LEAVES, CHOPPED
SESAME SEEDS, BLACK AND WHITE
AVOCADO, SLICED

DRESSING Mix all ingredients thoroughly and refrigerate until needed.

SALAD Combine all ingredients in large bowl and toss with dressing. Divide into co-op dishes (12 portions will fill up 3 rectangles or 4 rounds), garnish, and refrigerate until needed.

*See Special Ingredients for the Co-op Cook on page 155.

**See Shredding Cabbage on page 63.

***Daikon is a white to transparent Japanese radish the shape and size of a very large carrot. Cut extra daikon into the shape of carrot sticks to eat alone or with dressing for a tasty snack.

> The ginger and mango are wonderfully tasty surprises. It's a delight to make, serve, and eat.
>
> –Uma on Garden Lane

Serve with our Barbecue Pulled Pork (see page 88) or hoisin-marinated flank steak.

Arugula and Goat Cheese Salad with Lemon Vinaigrette

SERVES 12

WE LOVE THE PEPPERY FLAVOR OF ARUGULA AS A NICE CHANGE FROM SPINACH OR MIXED GREENS IN A SALAD. YOU CAN FIND IT IN MOST MAJOR SUPERMARKETS IN THE PACKAGED GREENS SECTION OF THE PRODUCE DEPARTMENT. ONE WAY TO KEEP THIS HARDY GREEN ON HAND ALL THE TIME IS TO GROW IT YOURSELF! IT'S MUCH EASIER TO GROW THAN ANY OTHER SALAD GREEN AND IS READY TO CLIP AND EAT IN A FEW WEEKS.

LEMON VINAIGRETTE

½   CUP FRESH LEMON JUICE

1   TEASPOON SALT

1   TEASPOON SUGAR

1   CUP OLIVE OIL
    PEPPER TO TASTE

SALAD

3   CUPS WALNUTS, CHOPPED AND
    TOASTED

1   HANDFUL ARUGULA LEAVES PER
    PERSON

8   OUNCES GOAT CHEESE

LEMON VINAIGRETTE Place lemon juice, salt, and sugar in a blender and slowly add olive oil in a thin stream while blending to emulsify the oil and juice. Add pepper to taste. Divide dressing among small serving containers for each family.

SALAD Divide walnuts into portions for each household. Divide the arugula greens among serving dishes. Slice cold goat cheese into thin rounds using Andy's method: Hold an 8-inch length of dental floss (non-mint flavored!) tautly in both hands to cut through the cheese without mushing each slice. Arrange the slices on top of the arugula.

> I love the flavor of the arugula with the walnuts, lemon, and goat cheese—just the right amount of pizzazz!
>
> –Lee on Riverview

This simple salad is the perfect accompaniment to our Salmon with Fresh Strawberry Relish or our Curried Carrot or Butternut Squash Soups (see pages 99, 80, and 81). Add a rustic loaf of bread and you've got a fantastic meal.

Uncover the formula that takes you way beyond lettuce and tomatoes

Change up the ingredients in your salads to suit the meal, the season, your mood, and what's available locally. After years of preparing salads for our dinner co-ops, we uncovered a secret formula you can follow to produce an exceptional salad every time. It's all in how you juxtapose these key flavors and textures: crunchy, sweet, tangy, and creamy. Include as many of the key flavors as you like, or you can make a salad that includes all complementary tastes.

Combine ingredients across the columns or from one or two columns, and you'll get something special every time.

GREENS	CRUNCHY	SWEET	TANGY	CREAMY	ADDITIONAL INGREDIENTS
Arugula	Nuts (toasted):	Nuts (sugared)**	Grapefruit	Avocado	Tomatoes
Spinach	almonds	Strawberries	Orange	Cheeses:	Bacon
Butter lettuce	pecans	Grapes	Pineapple	blue	Beets
Leaf Lettuce:	hazelnuts	Mandarin	Pomegranate	goat	Asparagus
red	walnuts	oranges	seeds	feta	Zucchini
green	pistachios	(canned)	Olives:	Parmesan	Green beans
Mustard greens	sunflower seeds	Dried fruit:	green	Asiago	Edible fresh
Sorrel	pine nuts	raisins	kalamata	Romano	flowers (no
Basil	peanuts	golden raisins	Radishes	mozzarella	pesticides)
Romaine	pumpkin seeds	currants	Red onion	Beans:	
Radicchio	Jicama	figs	Green onion	garbanzo	
Sprouts	Baby turnips	cranberries	Fried shallots	kidney	
Iceberg	Snap peas	dates		white	
	Cabbage	cherries		black	
	Bell peppers	apples		navy	
	Croutons*	pears		cannellini	
	Apples	mangoes		pinto	
	Carrots	berries			
	Celery	peaches			
	Radishes:				
	daikon				
	watermelon				
	red				

Salad Ingredient Combos

*See page 69 for Croutons recipe.
**See page 60 for Chile Maple Pecans recipe.

Salad Dressings

Homemade dressing isn't a requirement in most co-ops—we often agree to pull out our own favorites from the fridge. However, it's always good to have some tricks up your sleeve for when a particular dressing will really complement a given salad and/or the meal. Homemade salad dressings are easy to make and serve as an extra treat for your co-op.

Traditionally, salad dressing uses a 3 : 1 oil-to-vinegar ratio, while we prefer a 2 : 1 ratio for reduced fat and increased flavor. Choose one or more from the Creamy column to get your "2 parts," and use any of the Tangy ingredients for your "1 part." Add a little from the sweet column if the dressing is too tart, and then add from the herby or spicy columns to create a flavor that will complement the meal or your mood. To taste your creation, grab a lettuce leaf or carrot and dip. Add salt and pepper to balance out the flavor.

Expand your repertoire with these ingredients to invent exciting new dressings of your own.

CREAMY	TANGY	SWEET	HERBY	SPICY
Buttermilk	Citrus juices	Sugar	Rosemary	Horseradish
Cheese (see salad chart)	Vinegars:	Honey	Basil	Wasabi
Avocado	balsamic	Maple syrup	Chives	Shallots
Yogurt	rice	Agave nectar	Tarragon	Red onion
Mayonnaise	apple cider	Ketchup	Dill	Chile oil
Oil:	Fresh ginger			Chipotles in adobo sauce
olive	Lemongrass			Spicy paprika
grapeseed	Mustard			Curry
sesame	Wine			Salsa
hazelnut	Ketchup			
walnut	Olives:			
Beans (see salad chart)	green			
Garlic (raw & roasted)	kalamata			

Salad Dressing Flavor Options

Spinach and Edamame Soup with a Touch of Cream

SERVES 12

EDAMAME BEANS GIVE THIS LUSCIOUS FRESH SOUP A TWIST. A SMALL AMOUNT OF CRÈME FRAÎCHE MAKES IT DECADENT BUT NOT TOO RICH.

1	TABLESPOON OLIVE OIL
1	ONION, DICED
6	CLOVES GARLIC, MINCED
6	CARROTS, DICED
12	CUPS CHICKEN OR VEGETABLE BROTH
40	OUNCES FRESH SPINACH, LARGE STEMS REMOVED
¾	TEASPOON FRESHLY GROUND NUTMEG
⅓	CUP BUTTER, ROOM TEMPERATURE
⅓	CUP FLOUR
24	OUNCES SHELLED, FROZEN EDAMAME, THAWED
½	CUP CRÈME FRAÎCHE*
3	TABLESPOONS FRESH LEMON JUICE
	SALT AND PEPPER TO TASTE

GARNISH SUGGESTIONS

ITALIAN PARSLEY, CHOPPED
CRÈME FRAÎCHE, ½ CUP PER HOUSEHOLD (PACKAGE SEPARATELY)

Heat oil over medium heat in a large soup pot. Sauté onion in oil until translucent. Add garlic and stir for 1 minute.

Add carrots and broth to onions and garlic. Bring to a boil and simmer until carrots are tender.

Add spinach to broth and cook until spinach is just wilted and still bright green. You may need to add spinach in several batches, allowing each batch to cook down before adding more spinach. Remove soup from the heat and let it cool. Puree the soup with a handheld (immersion) blender or in batches in a blender or food processor until smooth. (Refrigerate if making ahead.) Return pureed soup to the soup pot over medium heat.

Combine nutmeg, butter, and flour in a small bowl to make a paste. Whisk this paste into the reheated soup and cook for 5 minutes.

Add edamame to the soup and simmer until barely tender and still bright green. Stir in the crème fraîche and lemon juice. Salt and pepper to taste. Divide soup among serving dishes.

*Crème fraîche can be found in the dairy or cheese section of markets, but it is easy to make if you remember to make it ahead of time: Combine 2 cups whipping cream with 4 tablespoons buttermilk in a glass container. Cover and let stand at room temperature (about 70 degrees F) from 8 to 24 hours, or until very thick. Stir well, cover, and refrigerate until you're ready to use (up to 10 days).

> I love the bright green color of this soup.
>
> –Debbie on 20th Street

Serve this soup with our Grilled Salmon Sandwich (see page 128) for a terrific complementary meal.

Roasted Asparagus Soup with Lemon

SERVES 12

HINTS OF BASIL, ZESTY LEMON, AND THE SUBTLE TANG OF GOAT CHEESE COMPLEMENT THE
ROASTED ASPARAGUS IN A FUSION OF SPRING FLAVORS. A RICH AND SATISFYING WEEKNIGHT SURPRISE.

ROASTED ASPARAGUS

6	POUNDS ASPARAGUS, TRIMMED, CUT IN 1-INCH PIECES
4	TABLESPOONS OLIVE OIL
	SALT AND PEPPER TO TASTE

SOUP

3	TABLESPOONS OLIVE OIL
6	LEEKS,* WHITE AND LIGHT GREEN PARTS ONLY, CHOPPED
2	SHALLOTS, CHOPPED
4	STALKS CELERY, CHOPPED
8	CUPS CHICKEN BROTH
1	LARGE RUSSET POTATO, PEELED AND DICED
1	CUP HALF-AND-HALF OR SOY CREAMER
8	OUNCES GOAT CHEESE, CRUMBLED
1	OUNCE FRESH BASIL LEAVES, CHOPPED
¼	CUP CHOPPED ITALIAN PARSLEY
1½	TABLESPOONS DIJON MUSTARD
1½	TEASPOONS FRESHLY GRATED NUTMEG
¼	CUP FRESH LEMON OR LIME JUICE
2	OUNCES FRESH CHIVES, CHOPPED

GARNISH SUGGESTIONS

SOUR CREAM
TOASTED PUMPKIN SEEDS
CROUTONS
LEMON SLICES

ROASTED ASPARAGUS Preheat oven to 425 degrees F. Toss olive oil, salt, and pepper with all of the asparagus, but keep the tips separate from the rest. Place on sheet pans (putting the tips on their own). Roast in oven for 15 minutes, rotating pans halfway through. Set aside until needed. The tips will be a garnish and will not be needed until the end.

SOUP In large soup pot, heat the olive oil on medium heat and add leeks and shallots until beginning to soften. Add celery and sauté for 5 more minutes.

Add broth and potatoes to leeks, bring to boil, and simmer until potatoes are fork tender, about 10 minutes.

With heat off, add ingredients from half-and-half through nutmeg to soup with the roasted asparagus (not tips). Puree the soup with a handheld (immersion) blender or in batches in a blender or food processor until smooth. Bring soup back up to temperature.

Stir lemon juice into soup. Divide into co-op dishes. Top with reserved asparagus tips and chopped chives.

*Washing Leeks: Leeks are one of those vegetables that can be hard to wash. We recommend the salad spinner method. After you have trimmed and cut the leeks according to the directions, place in the salad spinner colander and rinse several times. Use your hands to separate the pieces of leek stuck together. Then put the spinner together and whirl to dry.

Serve with our Swiss Chard Spanakopita with Feta. (see page 122).

Cumin Corn Soup with Red Peppers and Cilantro

SERVES 12

THIS SOUP IS TERRIFIC WITH A SALAD FOR A LIGHT MEAL, ESPECIALLY DURING SUMMER, THE SEASON FOR FRESH CORN ON THE COB. WE ADD THE CORNCOBS TO THE BROTH TO ADD AN EXTRA LAYER OF CORN FLAVOR. ELEVATE IT TO MAIN DISH STATUS BY ADDING YOUR FAVORITE SAUSAGE, CHUNKS OF SMOKED HAM, OR EVEN SOME CRUMBLED BACON JUST BEFORE SERVING.

12	EARS FRESH CORN, TRIMMED
1	TABLESPOON OLIVE OIL
1	LARGE ONION, DICED
1	TABLESPOON MINCED JALAPEÑO PEPPER
3	QUARTS CHICKEN OR VEGETABLE BROTH
1/4	CUP BUTTER, ROOM TEMPERATURE
1/4	CUP FLOUR
1	CUP HALF-AND-HALF OR SOY CREAMER
2	TEASPOONS WHOLE CUMIN, GROUND
	SALT TO TASTE

GARNISH SUGGESTIONS
(PACKAGE SEPARATELY)

CILANTRO, CHOPPED
RED BELL PEPPER, DICED

Cut corn kernels from the cobs and set both aside separately. Heat oil in a large soup pot over medium heat. Add onion and jalapeño, and sauté over medium heat until onion is translucent but not browned. Add broth and corncobs to the pot. Simmer for 30 minutes. Remove corncobs and discard.

Make a paste with butter and flour. Whisk this mixture into the corn broth and continue simmering corn broth for 10 minutes. In the meantime, puree $3/4$ of the corn kernels with $1^1/2$ cups of broth in a blender or food processor (in batches). Pour the puree through a strainer and into the corn broth.

Whisk half-and-half and cumin into the stock and add salt to taste. Divide remaining corn kernels (unprocessed) among serving dishes. Pour corn soup on top of raw corn kernels.

> **Red peppers and fresh green cilantro make a pretty presentation.**
>
> –Judy on Wildbrooke Court

Serve with our Tangy Spinach Salad or Caesar Salad (see pages 67 and 68) topped with grilled sausage.

Smoky Vegetable Lentil Soup with Spinach and Feta

SERVES 12

SMOKY SPANISH PAPRIKA AND THE FRUIT TASTES OF APPLE JUICE AND DRIED PEARS ADD COMPLEX FLAVOR TO THE LENTILS. SEND ALONG SOME GOOD WHOLE-GRAIN BREAD FROM YOUR FAVORITE BAKER AND A SIMPLE SALAD OF MIXED GREENS WITH OUR WHITE BALSAMIC VINAIGRETTE (SEE PAGE 141).

SMOKY ONIONS

3   TABLESPOONS OLIVE OIL
2   ONIONS, DICED
2   TABLESPOONS SMOKED PAPRIKA*
1½   TEASPOONS WHOLE CUMIN, GROUND
½   TEASPOON FRESHLY GRATED NUTMEG

LENTIL SOUP

6   CUPS CHICKEN OR VEGETABLE BROTH
6   CUPS WATER
2¼   CUPS APPLE JUICE
14   OUNCES CANNED CRUSHED TOMATOES*
28   OUNCES CANNED DICED TOMATOES*
3⅓   CUPS LENTILS, PICKED OVER AND RINSED
1½   CUPS DRIED PEARS, MINCED
2   STALKS CELERY, DICED
2   CARROTS, PEELED AND DICED
     SALT TO TASTE
8   OUNCES FRESH SPINACH, LARGE STEMS REMOVED, CHOPPED

GARNISH SUGGESTIONS
(PACKAGE SEPARATELY)

FETA, CRUMBLED

SMOKY ONIONS Heat oil over medium heat in large soup pot, add onions, and cook until almost translucent, about 10 minutes.

Add paprika, cumin, and nutmeg to onions and sauté for 2 minutes.

LENTIL SOUP Add liquids, tomatoes, lentils, and pears to the Smoky Onions and bring to a boil. Simmer, stirring occasionally, for 45 minutes.

Add celery, carrots, and salt to soup and simmer for 30 minutes.

Place spinach in the bottom of serving containers and ladle soup on top.

*See Special Ingredients for the Co-op Cook on page 155.

> Salty feta balances the sweetness of fruits and vegetables in this soup.
>
> –Sarah on 16th

For a non-vegetarian meal, add precooked sausage such as Gerhard's Chicken Apple Sausage—just slice, sauté, and serve on top.

Curried Carrot Soup with Sweet Potatoes

SERVES 12

GINGER AND COCONUT MILK . . . SOME OF OUR FAVORITE FLAVORS COMBINE INTO ONE COMFORTING SOUP THAT ARRIVES AT THE DOOR IN AN UNEXPECTED WAVE OF COLOR. THOUGH IT LOOKS AND TASTES SPECIAL ENOUGH FOR THE HOLIDAYS, WE RECOMMEND SPOILING YOUR CO-OP WITH THIS LOVELY SOUP ANY WEEKNIGHT OF THE YEAR.

GINGER MAPLE CREAM

- 1 CUP HALF-AND-HALF OR SOY CREAMER
- 2 INCHES GINGERROOT, PEELED AND SLICED IN ROUNDS
- 2 TABLESPOONS MAPLE SYRUP
- 1 CUP SOUR CREAM

CURRIED CARROT SOUP

- 2 TABLESPOONS OLIVE OIL
- 4 CUPS CHOPPED ONIONS
- 5 CLOVES GARLIC, MINCED
- 2 TABLESPOONS CURRY PASTE, OR TO TASTE* (MILD TO HOT DEPENDING ON PREFERENCE)
- 3 POUNDS CARROTS, PEELED AND CHOPPED
- 2½ POUNDS YAMS OR SWEET POTATOES, PEELED AND CHOPPED
- 7 CUPS CHICKEN BROTH
- 4 CUPS WATER
- 14 OUNCES CANNED COCONUT MILK
- ¼ CUP SMOOTH PEANUT BUTTER, WITHOUT ADDED SUGAR AND OTHER INGREDIENTS
- 2 TABLESPOONS MINCED FRESH GINGER
  SALT AND PEPPER TO TASTE

GARNISH SUGGESTIONS
(PACKAGE SEPARATELY)

  PECANS, CHOPPED

GINGER MAPLE CREAM Heat the half-and-half (or soy creamer) over low heat with the ginger and maple syrup for 10 minutes. Stir occasionally to keep skin from forming. Cool in refrigerator. Strain into sour cream and combine. Transfer into individual side dishes to send as a garnish.

CURRIED CARROT SOUP Heat oil over medium heat in a large soup pot and add onions; sauté for 5 to 10 minutes, until they begin to soften. Add the garlic and curry paste, and sauté 1 minute to release the curry spices.

Add carrots, yams, broth, and water to onion mixture and bring to a boil. Cook until vegetables are tender, about 15 to 20 minutes.

Add remaining ingredients to soup. Remove soup from heat. Puree soup with a handheld (immersion) blender or in batches in a blender or food processor until smooth. Return pureed soup to the soup pot over medium heat until heated through. Portion into co-op containers.

*See Special Ingredients for the Co-op Cook on page 155.

> I use a Japanese sweet potato, so the soup is a bright orange. Together with a dollop of stark white cream in the middle, it makes a beautiful splash on any holiday table.
>
> —Jennifer on 23rd Street

Serve this with our Wild Rice and Chickpea Salad (see page 147).

Butternut Squash Soup with Sage and Apples

Serves 12

IF YOU'VE EVER TASTED FRESH BUTTERNUT SQUASH RAVIOLI SERVED SIMPLY WITH BROWNED BUTTER AND SAGE, YOU'LL BE HOOKED ON THIS SOUP, WHICH IS AN EXTENSION OF ALL THOSE FLAVORS. IT'S THE MEAL YOU WANT TO COME IN TO AFTER AN AFTERNOON OF RAKING LEAVES. IF YOU WOULD LIKE TO GET STARTED AHEAD OF TIME, BAKE THE SQUASH AND MAKE THE FRIED SAGE LEAVES AND MAPLE CREAM EARLIER IN THE DAY.

FRIED SAGE LEAVES

⅓	CUP BUTTER
¾	OUNCE FRESH SAGE LEAVES

MAPLE CREAM

12	OUNCES SOUR CREAM
3	TABLESPOONS MAPLE SYRUP

BUTTERNUT SQUASH SOUP

7	POUNDS BUTTERNUT SQUASH
1–2	TABLESPOONS OLIVE OIL
2	SWEET ONIONS, CHOPPED (SUCH AS CANDY, WALLA WALLA, OR VIDALIA)
4½	TABLESPOONS BUTTER
¾	OUNCE FRESH SAGE LEAVES, CHOPPED
5	CLOVES GARLIC, MINCED
6	CUPS CHICKEN BROTH
1½	CUPS APPLE CIDER
1½	TEASPOONS SALT
	PEPPER TO TASTE
11	OUNCES WHOLE-MILK RICOTTA CHEESE
⅓	CUP ASIAGO CHEESE, GRATED

GARNISH SUGGESTIONS
(PACKAGE SEPARATELY)

DRIED APPLE CHIPS*
OR CURRIED CASHEWS**

FRIED SAGE LEAVES Melt butter in small sauté pan over low heat and sauté sage until crisp but still green, about 10 to 15 minutes. Stir occasionally so that sage and butter don't burn. Remove sage leaves and let cool. Use remaining butter as part of the butter to sauté the onions. The fried sage leaves will be a garnish; package separately for each household.

MAPLE CREAM Mix and put in separate containers for each family. (Place in refrigerator until needed.) This will also be a garnish.

BUTTERNUT SQUASH SOUP Preheat oven to 450 degrees F.

Cut squash in half lengthwise and seed. Place on sheet pans and brush them lightly with olive oil. Roast for 50 minutes until tender. Let cool. Scoop out flesh and set aside. (Refrigerate if making ahead.)

Sauté onions in butter over medium heat in soup pot until onions are translucent. Add fresh sage and garlic to onions and continue to sauté for 5 minutes. Add broth, cider, salt, and pepper along with butternut squash to onions and bring to a boil, stirring occasionally. Reduce heat to low and simmer 5 minutes.

Stir cheeses into soup and puree the soup with a handheld (immersion) blender or in batches in a blender or food processor until smooth. Portion out into co-op containers.

*Apple chips are dried apples, dried even more. Our favorite local apple chips are Uncle Lou's, who adds cinnamon and makes them nice and thick. They are also made like potato chips by national brands such as Seneca. Regular dried apples are not a good substitute; if you can't find apple chips, omit them.

**Curried nuts are another wonderful topping for this soup. We like curried cashews, which you can find in a supermarket with a good bulk section.

If you would like to make this soup even heartier, you may add sautéed sliced sausage at the end. Our Tangy Spinach Salad will round out the meal nicely (see page 67).

Alex's Crab Corn Chowder

SERVES 12

DECADENT ENOUGH FOR A SPECIAL DINNER PARTY, BUT EASY TO WHIP UP ON A WEDNESDAY AFTER WORK, THIS CHOWDER MAKES PEOPLE HAPPY. FIRST SERVED BY AUNT SUE ON CHRISTMAS EVE IN ATLANTA, IT WAS A FLAVOR COMBINATION ALEX COULDN'T FORGET. IF YOU'RE COOKING FOR A BUNCH OF HEDONISTS, INDULGE WITH CREAM IN PLACE OF SOME OF THE MILK, OR IF YOU WANT TO MAKE IT SPICY, ADD MORE OLD BAY.

2	TABLESPOONS OLIVE OIL
4	TABLESPOONS BUTTER
2	LARGE ONIONS, DICED
3	STALKS CELERY, DICED
3	RUSSET OR YUKON GOLD POTATOES, PEELED AND DICED
1	RED BELL PEPPER, DICED
2	TABLESPOONS OLD BAY SEASONING*
1/3	CUP FLOUR
6	CUPS CHICKEN BROTH
6	CUPS WHOLE MILK
32	OUNCES FROZEN CORN
1½	POUNDS COOKED LUMP CRABMEAT**
	SALT AND PEPPER TO TASTE
12	SMALL BREAD BOWLS (LARGE SOURDOUGH ROLLS) OR SERVE WITH SEASONED BREADSTICKS OR SOURDOUGH BAGUETTES

GARNISH SUGGESTION

PARSLEY, CHOPPED

In a large soup pot, swirl in olive oil and melt the butter. Add onions and celery, and cook on medium for 10 minutes, or until soft. Add potatoes and red pepper, and cook for 3 more minutes, stirring occasionally. Stir in Old Bay. Sprinkle in flour and stir constantly for two minutes. Stir in chicken broth and milk. Once it begins to bubble, add corn. Simmer for 5 minutes and then turn off heat. Puree about a third of the soup with a hand-held blender or in blender or food processor and then return soup to the pot. Be sure and leave some of the corn and potatoes whole so they're still recognizable.

At the very last minute, fold in the lump crabmeat and warm it through. Stir minimally, trying to keep some of the lumps intact. Taste the soup and add salt and pepper as needed.

Precut the bread bowls by pointing the knife down and working it around in a circle. You may need to gently tear at the inside to hollow it out, leaving a thick wall of bread. Deliver bowls with their "cores" back in. Families will then serve individual portions of soup in each bowl. It's a fun presentation and a bona fide hit with kids.

> The baker at my supermarket offered to make my bread bowls fresh for me while I did my shopping. She had them ready for me in fifteen minutes. It's a trick worth repeating.
>
> –Vida on Berkeley Street

*Old Bay is the perfect seasoning for crab and gives this chowder a distinctive kick. It's easy to find Old Bay in its yellow and blue tin at the fish counter or in the spice aisle.

**You can often find cartons of fresh lump crabmeat at a supermarket's fish counter, frozen crab at a seafood market, or "fancy lump crabmeat" in a can at a gourmet store.

This chowder is surprisingly forgiving and versatile. Try spinning it southwestern—leave out the Old Bay and use poblano and jalapeño peppers. Garnish with cilantro or sliced green onions, and you've got a totally different dish.

Asian Chard Soup with Goat Cheese Crostini

Serves 12

This could be called Immunity Soup! Miso contains trace minerals that help strengthen the immune system. Shiitake mushrooms have medicinal properties to fight viruses, and seaweed is packed with minerals. If you don't care about any of that, eat it because it tastes so good. The Goat Cheese Crostini is great with any soup.

Leek Ginger Broth

- 3 TABLESPOONS OLIVE OIL
- 3 LEEKS,* WHITE AND LIGHT GREEN PARTS, CHOPPED
- 6 CLOVES GARLIC, CHOPPED
- 4 CUPS CHICKEN BROTH
- 3 (6-INCH) PIECES DRIED JAPANESE SEAWEED (KOMBU**)
- 3 INCHES FRESH GINGER, PEELED AND SLICED INTO THICK ROUNDS

Soup

- 32 OUNCES FIRM TOFU, DRAINED***
- 3 TABLESPOONS OLIVE OIL
- 2 BUNCHES SWISS CHARD, LEAVES AND STEMS DICED SEPARATELY****
- 2 CUPS SLICED SHIITAKE MUSHROOMS
- 4 CUPS WATER (OR MORE IF SOUP IS TOO THICK)
- ¾ CUP MISO PASTE, ANY KIND (DARK MISO WILL ADD RICH COLOR)
- 1 CUP HOT WATER
- 1½ TEASPOONS CHILE OIL, OR TO TASTE

Goat Cheese Crostini

- 3 BAGUETTES, SLICED
- ½ HEAD GARLIC, SEPARATED FROM HEAD BUT NOT PEELED
- ½ CUP OLIVE OIL
- 12 OUNCES GOAT CHEESE

Leek Ginger Broth Heat oil over medium heat in a medium pot (use a soup pot when you get to the chard). Add leeks and garlic, and sauté until translucent.

Add broth, kombu, and ginger to leeks, bring to boil, and simmer for 10 minutes. Remove from heat and discard kombu and ginger. Puree the soup with a handheld (immersion) blender or in batches in a blender or food processor until smooth. Set aside until needed.

Soup Dice tofu into ¼-inch cubes and set aside.

Heat olive oil in large soup pot. Add diced chard **ribs,** chard **stems** and mushrooms; sauté until cooked, about 10 minutes. Add homemade broth and water; bring to boil. Lower heat, add chard **leaves,** and simmer 10 minutes. Add more water if needed. Add drained and diced tofu.

In a small bowl, mix miso paste with hot water until combined. Add to soup with chile oil and simmer gently for 10 minutes. Divide into co-op dishes.

Goat Cheese Crostini Preheat broiler. Place sliced bread on cookie sheets and toast for 1 minute on each side, or until brown. This is easy to do in batches. Cool. Repackage (in baguette bags) to serve to co-op.

> The goat cheese spread tastes GREAT! It's really sour.
>
> –Mae, age 5

Cook garlic in nonstick pan on medium heat for 10 minutes to "dry roast" until soft; turn occasionally. Cool. Peel and then puree with olive oil in food processor. Add goat cheese to processor and puree. Divide into separate side containers for delivery. To eat, slather onto sliced toasted bread and enjoy.

*See Washing Leeks Technique on page 76.

**Kombu is a wonderful flavoring for soups. Find it in bulk or in packages in the Asian section of a good grocery store or at an Asian market.

***To drain tofu, place on a plate and stack another plate on top. Weight with something heavy like a book or a can. Let tofu rest for one hour and then drain off water. Draining the water from tofu will let it soak in the flavor of what you're cooking.

****Showing Chard Who's Boss: Chard might be the biggest, most unruly ingredient to enter our kitchens. Don't be afraid of it—instead, show it who's boss. Chopping chard is a technique worth mastering if you want to become friends with one of the world's healthiest foods. First, cut off the large chard stems where they join the leaf and set them aside. Stems can be cut (as per recipe) and sautéed right along with onions in any recipe to add beautiful color and texture—they take longer to cook than the leaves do. Wash the leaves; no need to dry them. Fold them lengthwise along the main midrib and cut this large rib out (ribs the diameter of a pencil or smaller can be left in). Combine the large ribs with the stems and use together with the stems in the recipe. Next stack 6 to 8 leaf halves and slice across the leaves, making strips about 1 inch wide and $2^{1}/_{2}$ to 3 inches long. If the strips are longer than 3 inches, cut them in half. If you need to dice the chard leaves, turn strips and dice.

Tacos à la Carte

SERVES 12

THIS IS AN ALL-OUT FUN MEAL—EVERYTHING IS SERVED À LA CARTE, SO EVEN THE PICKIEST EATERS WILL FIND SOMETHING THEY LIKE. IF YOU'VE BEEN LOOKING FOR A STANDBY RECIPE FOR GROUND BEEF TO USE WITH BURRITOS OR TACOS, YOU MAY HAVE FOUND IT. TO GO DELUXE, SERVE WITH RICE AND BEANS. HAVE FUN!

À LA CARTE ELEMENTS

ROMA TOMATOES, CHOPPED
LETTUCE, SHREDDED
CHEESE, GRATED
SALSA, FROM A JAR OR HOMEMADE
SOUR CREAM
TACO SHELLS, 2 PER PERSON
TORTILLA CHIPS

GUACAMOLE

4	LARGE AVOCADOES
7	OUNCES CANNED SALSA VERDE
1	TABLESPOON FRESH LIME JUICE*
3	CLOVES GARLIC, MINCED
	SALT TO TASTE
	CILANTRO, DICED (OPTIONAL)

GROUND BEEF TACO FILLING

3	TABLESPOONS OLIVE OIL
3	POUNDS GROUND BEEF OR GROUND TURKEY
1	LARGE ONION, DICED
6	CLOVES GARLIC, MINCED
10	OUNCES CANNED SALSA VERDE
3	TABLESPOONS FRESH LIME JUICE
1	TEASPOON GROUND WHOLE CUMIN
	PINCH FRESHLY GRATED NUTMEG
	PASILLA OR ANCHO CHILE POWDER* TO TASTE

À LA CARTE ELEMENTS Package these separately for the buffet.

GUACAMOLE Mash everything together and take a taste with a chip. Add more salsa verde, lime juice, or salt as needed. Package individually with a pit in each container, and gently press cling wrap onto the surface of the guacamole to keep out air and maintain color. The lime juice also helps guacamole stay a pretty green. Refrigerate until delivering meals.

GROUND BEEF TACO FILLING Heat oil in large pan and add ground beef. Stir as it browns for 2 to 3 minutes. Add onion and garlic to ground beef and stir until cooked through, about 3 to 5 minutes. Add remaining ingredients to beef and onion, and cook until heated. Place in co-op dishes.

BEANS (OPTIONAL)—Make your favorite refried bean recipe or just heat some canned beans for this dish. If you use the canned beans, add a few extras like fire-roasted diced tomatoes,* minced garlic, and ground cumin to add some flavor.

RICE (OPTIONAL) Make your favorite simple rice. Jasmine rice made in the microwave is always an easy trick. To make it a little more flavorful, add some of your favorite salsa and mix it together before placing it in serving dishes. You will not need a ton of rice for this, so plan on using 2 cups of dry rice for 12 servings.

*See Special Ingredients for the Co-op Cook on page 155.

> A fiesta for the whole family—my kids love to assemble tacos by themselves. And this is some of the best guac I've ever tasted.
>
> –Sarah on 16th Street

To make taco filling spicier, add diced jalapeños, more pasilla powder, or pureed canned chipotle peppers in adobo sauce.

Barbecue Pulled Pork in the Crockpot

SERVES 12

HERE IS AN EASY CROWD-PLEASER YOU CAN START AHEAD OF TIME. START OVERNIGHT IN THE CROCKPOT, PULL IT OUT IN THE MORNING, SHRED IT, ADD BARBECUE SAUCE, AND PUT IT BACK IN THE CROCKPOT.

2 ONIONS, SLICED
6 POUNDS PORK SHOULDER*
2 CUPS WATER
3 CUPS BARBECUE SAUCE, USE ONE OF OURS** OR YOUR FAVORITE

Place onion slices in slow cooker.*** Lay cut of pork on top of onions. If it does not fit well, cut it into 2 to 4 smaller chunks. Pour water over. Set on low and cook overnight, up to 12 hours.

In the morning, use a barbecue fork and a spatula or tongs to pull out the pork and rest on a sheet pan(s). Discard the water. Use tongs, a fork, or clean fingers to shred the pork; it will shred easily but will be hot. Separate fat and discard. Keep the onions with the meat if you like. Combine shredded pork with barbecue sauce and cook on low for another 4 to 6 hours. (If you are late eaters, refrigerate pork in the barbecue sauce for a few hours before the second cooking.) After the barbecue has cooked for 4 hours, stir for even cooking. The pork will be ready to go directly into the co-op dishes from the crockpot.

*The pork shoulder is usually sold in two large cuts. The top part is called a Boston butt or pork butt. The lower section is called a picnic ham or picnic shoulder. Either one will work well for this recipe. The shoulder is a fatty cut and so may be cooked for a long time. We use a larger portion of meat for this recipe than usual because you lose fat in the cooking process and end up with a smaller portion.

**Barbecue Sauce: See our recipe for Jock's Mustard Barbecue Sauce and our Dijon-Apricot Barbecue Sauce (see pages 92 and 93). Both work well. (Our recipe makes 5 1/2 cups.)

***Slow cookers come in many sizes. We use a newer one that's 8 quarts and works great for co-op meals. If you have a smaller one and are cooking more than 6 pounds of pork, borrow another slow cooker from a friend for the overnight cooking.

Serve as sandwiches with fresh-baked rolls and our Ginger Apple Coleslaw (see page 70) or serve with cornbread and beans.

Lamb Chops with Mint-Orange Crust

SERVES 12

LAMB IS A SPECIAL TREAT WHEN PRESENTED ON A WEEKNIGHT. WHEN YOU COME ACROSS REALLY NICE LAMB CHOPS, EVERYONE IN YOUR CO-OP CAN HIT THE JACKPOT. PORTION ONE CHOP PER PERSON AND THE DINNER WILL SEEM LAVISH WHILE STILL BEING AFFORDABLE.

24 CLOVES GARLIC, SEPARATED BUT NOT PEELED

¾ CUP PINE NUTS, TOASTED

¾ OUNCE FRESH MINT LEAVES

3 ORANGES, ZESTED AND JUICED (JUICE RESERVED)

¼ CUP OLIVE OIL

12 LAMB CHOPS (ABOUT 1 INCH THICK—OR ADJUST COOKING TIME)
SALT AND PEPPER
OLIVE OIL

GARNISH SUGGESTIONS

ASPARAGUS RIBBONS*
ORANGES, SLICED
FRESH MINT LEAVES

Cook garlic in a nonstick pan on medium heat for 10 minutes to "dry roast" until soft; turn occasionally. Cool and then peel.

Put peeled garlic in a food processor and process until finely minced. Add pine nuts, mint, and orange zest; process until combined. Slowly drizzle in olive oil.

Allow lamb to rest at room temperature for 30 minutes before cooking. Generously salt and pepper both sides of chops. Place a large spoonful of mint pesto on top of each piece of lamb and spread evenly with a spoon. Cover two skillets (or bottom of a large heavy-duty roasting pan over two burners) with a thin layer of olive oil and bring to medium heat. When pan is hot but not smoking, place chops in, pesto side down, and sauté for 6 minutes. Turn chops over with a spatula and/or tongs and cook for 8 minutes. Add reserved orange juice, cover, lower heat to medium-low, and cook until done, 2 to 5 minutes. (You may test for done-ness by cutting into a chop. It should still be pink but not blood red if you like it medium-rare. Remember, they will continue to cook after they are out of the pan.) Transfer to serving dishes.

> Lamb with built-in mint jelly—orange juice and mint make the perfect flavor pairing.
>
> –Sarah on 16th Street

*Making Asparagus Ribbons: Asparagus ribbons are a festive raw garnish you may use for many dishes. Slice asparagus very thinly lengthwise using a mandolin. You can also use a vegetable peeler, which is a little trickier: Lay one asparagus stalk at a time on a cutting board and run peeler from the base of the stalk to the top, cutting long ribbons. (You may have to place the asparagus on the edge of the cutting board to accommodate your hand and the handle of the peeler.)

Serve with our Cauliflower Clouds with Julienne Brussels Sprouts (see page 138).

Sun-Dried Tomato Meatloaf with Basil

SERVES 12 (3 LOAF PANS)

THIS IS NOT YOUR MAMA'S MEATLOAF! BASIL AND SUN-DRIED TOMATOES ADD SURPRISE TO THIS CLASSIC COMFORT FOOD. ROUND OUT THE MEAL WITH SAUTÉED VEGETABLES OR A SPINACH SALAD. IT MAKES A KILLER SANDWICH THE NEXT DAY. JUST SLICE THE COLD MEATLOAF AND SAUTÉ BOTH SIDES IN A PAN. ADD YOUR FAVORITE CHEESE AND TOAST SOME SOURDOUGH BREAD, AND YOU'RE IN FOR SOMETHING SPECIAL.

MUSHROOM-WINE INFUSION

1	LARGE ONION, QUARTERED
1	TABLESPOON OLIVE OIL
8	OUNCES CREMINI MUSHROOMS
6	CLOVES GARLIC, MINCED
2/3	CUP RED WINE

PUTTING MEATLOAF TOGETHER

6	EGGS
16	OUNCES V8 VEGETABLE JUICE
2	TABLESPOONS WORCESTERSHIRE SAUCE
2	TABLESPOONS DIJON MUSTARD
1	TABLESPOON BALSAMIC VINEGAR
2	TEASPOONS PEPPER
3/4	TEASPOON SALT
3/4	CUP SUN-DRIED TOMATOES, PACKED IN OIL, DRAINED AND CHOPPED
4	ROASTED RED PEPPERS, FROM A JAR OR HOMEMADE, DICED
3	OUNCES FRESH BASIL LEAVES, CHOPPED
1½	CUPS CHEDDAR CHEESE, GRATED
4½	CUPS WHOLE-WHEAT BREAD CRUMBS, HOMEMADE*
5	POUNDS GROUND MEAT**

MUSHROOM-WINE INFUSION Puree onions in food processor. Heat olive oil in sauté pan on medium-low heat. Add onions and sauté until translucent, about 5 to 10 minutes. Clean and trim ends of mushrooms. Puree in food processor. Add to onion mix and continue to cook for 5 minutes. Add minced garlic and cook 1 minute. Add wine and reduce until no longer "wet," about 10 minutes. Cool Mushroom-Wine Infusion.

PUTTING MEATLOAF TOGETHER Spray loaf pans with nonstick spray and place on a sheet pan.

Preheat oven to 425 degrees F.

Whisk ingredients from eggs through salt in a large bowl. Add remaining ingredients to egg mixture along with Mushroom-Wine Infusion. Roll up your sleeves and mix with clean hands. For meatloaf, it seems to be the best method. Then parcel out evenly into prepared pans, shaping high and rounded like a loaf of bread just out of oven. Bake on center rack for 1 hour, or until meat is no longer pink. Cover with foil and deliver.

*Making Bread Crumbs: Tear leftover whole-wheat bread into pieces (defrost if frozen) and place in food processor. Process until they are uniform crumbs. Toast on a sheet pan in the oven at 200 degrees F until they have dried out, about 10 minutes. Stir carefully halfway through. (If you will be placing bread crumbs directly on top of the food and baking longer, you do not need to brown them in the oven for very long.)

**We like to use a combination of ground beef, lamb, pork, and turkey for a wonderful flavor. You can also really tell the difference when you use quality grass-fed meat.

This meatloaf recipe also produces some tasty meatballs. Shape meat into 2-inch balls, place on a sheet pan sprayed with cooking spray, and bake at 375 degrees F until brown and cooked through, about 20 minutes.

Jock's Country-Style Ribs with Two Mustard Barbecue Sauces

SERVES 12

ALEX'S DAD, JOCK, MAKES THESE TENDER CAYENNE-RUBBED RIBS FOR LUCKY VISITORS TO THE HOUSE ON LYMAN LAKE, SOUTH CAROLINA. HIS DISTINCT METHOD OF OVEN ROASTING WITH A LITTLE WATER IS THE SECRET TO KEEPING THE RIBS MOIST. WE BRING YOU TWO OPTIONS: JOCK'S SHARP MUSTARDY SAUCE THAT USES WHAT A SOUTHERN GUY'S GOT IN HIS PANTRY OR CHEF ANDY'S SOPHISTICATED SPIN WITH APRICOT AND DIJON.

18　COUNTRY-STYLE BONELESS
　　PORK RIBS* (1½ LARGE RIBS
　　PER PERSON)
　　SALT AND PEPPER
　　CAYENNE PEPPER, IN A SHAKER
　　WATER

JOCK'S MUSTARD BARBECUE SAUCE (MAKES 5½ CUPS)

¾　CUP HONEY
⅓　CUP APPLE CIDER VINEGAR
⅓　CUP MOLASSES
2　TEASPOONS CANOLA OIL
¾　TEASPOON DRIED OREGANO
¾　TEASPOON DRIED THYME
¾　TEASPOON PEPPER
¼　TEASPOON CAYENNE PEPPER

1　CUP CORN SYRUP (KARO)
24　OUNCES YELLOW MUSTARD

Preheat oven to 300 degrees F.

Line workspace with wax paper or parchment paper. Pat ribs dry with paper towels. Sprinkle both sides with salt and pepper to taste and dust lightly all over with cayenne. Transfer to wire racks over cookie sheets, broiler pans, or a combination of the two—no ribs touching. (If you need another pan or rack, borrow one from a neighbor because these must all go into the oven at one time.) Add ⅓ cup of water to each pan and roast in oven for 90 minutes, turning once at the 45-minute mark.

With 10 minutes to go, place barbecue sauce in a saucepan on low and bring to a simmer.

At the end of cooking time, take the ribs out of oven and preheat broiler. Brush ribs liberally with the barbecue sauce. In batches, run them under the hot broiler for a few minutes, turning to crisp up the outsides all over. (No more than 5 minutes under the broiler or they will dry out.) Cover the bottom of co-op containers with warm barbecue sauce; nestle ribs in. You will have plenty of sauce left over to serve on the side.

*Bone-in ribs work just as well but take up more space in the oven per serving.

JOCK'S MUSTARD BARBECUE SAUCE Combine all ingredients in a blender and blend until smooth. Refrigerate until needed. (May be made ahead of time.)

If you are fortunate enough to live in the South, Jock recommends skipping all the work and buying Maurice's Carolina Gold Mustard Barbecue Sauce, also available online.

Serve with our Ginger Apple Coleslaw (see page 70) and local corn on the cob.

DIJON-APRICOT BARBECUE SAUCE

REPLACE CORN SYRUP WITH
8   OUNCES APRICOT FRUIT SPREAD**
REPLACE YELLOW MUSTARD WITH
24 OUNCES DIJON MUSTARD

GARNISH SUGGESTIONS

KALE
FRESH THYME SPRIGS
FRESH OREGANO SPRIGS

DIJON-APRICOT BARBECUE SAUCE Combine all ingredients from Jock's Mustard Barbecue Sauce recipe in a blender, replacing corn syrup and yellow mustard as listed, and blend until smooth. Refrigerate until needed.

**Pick a flavor of a smooth jam, jelly, or all-fruit spread, such as pomegranate, plum, or orange cranberry. If you make jellies or jams, this is the place to highlight your craft.

MAKE IT CHICKEN You will like this easy barbecue sauce so much you won't want to stop with ribs. Lightly coat chicken and cook on the grill. Warm a little barbecue sauce to coat the bottom of the pan and serve with some extra on the side as a dipping sauce. (Be careful to keep the sauce you use for the raw chicken separate from remaining barbecue sauce.) When using apricot jam, Andy likes quickly grilling fresh apricot halves for 1 to 2 minutes to serve on top of the chicken as a tasty garnish. You'll also need a little color for the chicken, so use a garnish suggestion.

> As I was reheating these at work, I had about six people come over and ask what the incredible smell was. I gave them a taste, and they were offering me money to trade them for their PB&Js!
>
> –Chrissy on 19th Street

Pesto Pasta with Pine Nuts and Smoked Trout

SERVES 12

THIS WONDERFUL SUMMER DISH COMES TOGETHER EASILY AND PLEASES EVERYONE, FROM PIZZA LOVERS TO CONNOISSEURS OF HAUTE CUISINE. IF YOU'VE BEEN GROWING BASIL, NOW IS YOUR MOMENT TO SHINE! IT'S ALSO A GREAT EXCUSE TO VISIT THE FARMERS' MARKET. TO KEEP PESTO GREEN AND COLORFUL, WE DISH THE PESTO ON TOP OF THE PASTA RATHER THAN MIXING IT IN.

BASIL PESTO SAUCE

4	OUNCES FRESH BASIL LEAVES
1½	CUPS PARMESAN OR ASIAGO, GRATED
1	CUP PINE NUTS, TOASTED
3	TABLESPOONS BUTTER
12	CLOVES GARLIC, MINCED
½	CUP OLIVE OIL

PASTA

¼	CUP SALT
2	POUNDS ASPARAGUS, TRIMMED AND CUT IN ½-INCH PIECES (KEEP TIPS WHOLE)
24	OUNCES WHOLE-WHEAT SPAGHETTI
⅓	CUP OLIVE OIL
16	OUNCES FROZEN SHELLED EDAMAME, THAWED
3	ROASTED RED PEPPERS FROM A JAR OR HOMEMADE, DICED
1½	POUNDS SMOKED TROUT,* SKIN REMOVED

GARNISH SUGGESTIONS
(CHOOSE YOUR FAVORITES)

CHERRY TOMATOES, HALVED
PARMESAN, SHAVED
PINE NUTS, TOASTED
FRESH BASIL LEAVES, CHOPPED
LEMON WHEELS

BASIL PESTO SAUCE Place all of the pesto ingredients, except the olive oil, in the food processor and pulse until roughly chopped. With motor running, slowly drizzle olive oil in from the top tube and process until well combined. Set aside. May be prepared one day ahead and refrigerated. If made ahead, pour a small amount of olive oil on top of pesto to keep fresh and green.

PASTA Fill a large pot with water and bring to a boil. Add salt and asparagus. Cook for 2 minutes. Strain and rinse with cold water to stop cooking. Set aside until needed.

In a large pot, cook pasta according to package directions. Drain and toss with olive oil. Divide into rectangle co-op dishes, making a little divot down the center.

In a large bowl, combine the pesto with the asparagus, edamame, and red peppers. Spoon a thick stripe of the pesto and vegetables over the pasta in the divot you've made.

Break the trout into large chunks and place it on either side of the "stripe" of pesto.

*Smoked trout has a rich, subtle flavor and is ready to eat. Look for it in the specialty meats department of the grocer or at the fish market. You may substitute smoked salmon.

> I love making this for my co-op. It's fun to arrange colorful displays of vegetables over steaming hot dishes of comforting spaghetti. Wow!
>
> –Jennifer on 23rd Street

Broiled Tuna with Miso, Lime, and Ginger Sauce

SERVES 12

HONEY, LIME, AND GINGER HARMONIZE TO COMPLEMENT FRESH AHI STEAKS. BROILING MAKES PREPARATION QUICK AND EASY. THE MARINADE AND GLAZE COMBINE TO KEEP THE FISH MOIST, EVEN WHEN REHEATED. ALSO TRY THIS MARINADE/GLAZE COMBO TO BRING OUT THE DELICATE FLAVORS OF TROUT AND SNAPPER. ADJUST COOKING TIMES DEPENDING ON THE THICKNESS OF THE FISH.

MISO MARINADE

- ½ CUP RED MISO
- ¼ CUP MIRIN (SWEET JAPANESE WINE)
- 2 TABLESPOONS FRESH LIME JUICE*
- 3 TABLESPOONS OLIVE OIL
- 1½ TEASPOONS ROASTED RED CHILE PASTE (FOUND IN THE ASIAN OR INDIAN FOODS GROCERY SECTION)
- 3 POUNDS AHI TUNA STEAKS

LIME AND GINGER GLAZE

- ½ CUP HONEY
- ½ CUP FRESH LIME JUICE*
- 3 TABLESPOONS TRIPLE SEC
- 3 TABLESPOONS GRATED FRESH GINGER*
- 1 TABLESPOON MINCED LEMONGRASS**
- 1½ LIMES, ZESTED

GARNISH SUGGESTIONS

- FRESH CHIVE STRANDS
- BLACK SESAME SEEDS
- LIMES, SLICED

MISO MARINADE Combine marinade ingredients in a small bowl.

Pour marinade over ahi tuna steaks. Cover and chill for 30 minutes.

LIME AND GINGER GLAZE Combine all glaze ingredients except lime zest and heat in a small saucepan over low heat until sauce thinly coats the back of a spoon. This will take about 10 minutes. Keep the glaze warm while the tuna broils.

Preheat broiler.

Lightly oil a broiler pan and broil tuna about 2 minutes per side for rare and 3 minutes for medium-rare. Let tuna steaks rest for 5 minutes, covered, then slice into portions and divide among serving dishes.

Stir lime zest into glaze. Pour glaze over each portion of tuna.

*See Special Ingredients for the Co-op Cook on page 155.

**Lemongrass Stalks: Be sure to peel off the tough outer layers and only chop the softer inner layers. As a shortcut, we also love Gourmet Garden brand Lemongrass Puree in a 4-ounce tube. It has a wonderful fresh taste and can be easier to find than lemongrass stalks. Look for it in the produce section near the fresh herbs.

> **Everybody raves about the sauce!**
>
> –Irwin on Garden Lane

Serve with our Asian Noodle Slaw (see page 63). The light tangy dressing and crunchy vegetables create a terrific balance of flavors, colors, and texture.

Vida's Pan-Fried Pecan Tilapia

SERVES 12

TILAPIA IS A MILD AND VERSATILE FISH THAT CAN BE USED IN A VARIETY OF PREPARATIONS. WE USE IT HERE IN PLACE OF CATFISH—IT HAS FEWER PIN BONES, AND THE SMALLER FILLET SIZES ARE WELL SUITED TO CO-OP PORTIONS. A SUPERB RECIPE TO CHOOSE IF YOU'RE SHORT ON COOKING TIME BUT STILL WANT TO MAKE A GREAT IMPRESSION.

1   CUP CORNMEAL (FINE-GROUND, NOT POLENTA)
¾   CUP PECANS
1   TABLESPOON SALT
1   TEASPOON PEPPER
4   POUNDS TILAPIA FILLETS (ONE 4- TO 6-OUNCE FILLET FOR EACH PERSON)
¾   CUP CANOLA OIL, DIVIDED

GARNISH SUGGESTIONS

LEMON WEDGES
ITALIAN PARSLEY SPRIGS

Combine cornmeal, pecans, salt, and pepper in a food processor until nuts are finely ground.

Dredge fish in cornmeal mixture to completely coat both sides.

Heat 3 tablespoons of oil in each of 2 nonstick sauté pans (or griddles) over medium-high heat. Cook 3 to 4 fish fillets in each pan until golden brown on both sides and barely firm to the touch. Remove fillets and place in serving dishes; keep warm while you cook remaining fish. Wipe out both pans and cook remaining fillets in the same manner.

> A quick and simple crowd-pleaser.
>
> –Sarah on 16th Street

Serve this flavorful fish atop a bed of rice seasoned with herbs and our Ginger Apple Coleslaw or our Tangy Spinach Salad and Roasted Sweet Potatoes with Orange Chipotle Glaze (see pages 70, 67, and 140).

Salmon with Fresh Strawberry Relish

SERVES 12

HERE'S A LIGHT AND HEALTHY MEAL WITH SOME SERIOUS VISUAL IMPACT. YOUR LUCKY RECEIVERS WILL OPEN UP THE LID TO A JUBILANT EXPLOSION OF COLOR AND FLAVOR—BRIGHT ORANGE SALMON AND A RAINBOW RELISH OF STRAWBERRIES, TARRAGON, AND BELL PEPPERS. ALL THE TASTES OF SUMMER ARE GORGEOUS TO BEHOLD.

STRAWBERRY RELISH

1½ PINTS STRAWBERRIES, DICED

1½ YELLOW BELL PEPPERS, DICED

4 GREEN ONIONS, GREEN AND WHITE PARTS, SLICED

3 TABLESPOONS FRESH TARRAGON, MINCED

⅓ CUP MAPLE SYRUP

SALT AND PEPPER TO TASTE

SALMON

4 POUNDS SALMON FILLETS

2 TABLESPOONS OLIVE OIL

SALT AND PEPPER TO TASTE

1 HANDFUL SPINACH OR ARUGULA PER FAMILY

GARNISH SUGGESTION

LEMONS, SLICED

STRAWBERRY RELISH Combine and mix well in a medium bowl. Allow to rest at room temperature 30 minutes to blend the flavors.

SALMON Preheat grill to 450 degrees F or preheat broiler.

Brush each fillet with oil and sprinkle with salt and pepper. Grill or broil fillets with the skin side down (if it has skin) until flesh just begins to flake.

Place one handful of greens in the bottom of each serving dish. Divide the portions of salmon and place them on top of greens. Spoon the relish over the salmon.

For a completely different grilled salmon dish, swap out the Strawberry Relish for our Lemon Wasabi Sauce on page 128.

> Sarah once paired this with Fresh Green Beans in Orange Vinaigrette—it was Christmas in July.
>
> –Alex on 10th Street

Serve with our Mango Basmati with Mint and Ginger (see page 151).

Snapper en Papillote with Carrots and Leeks

SERVES 12

WHEN YOU SEE "EN PAPILLOTE" ON A MENU, IT MEANS THE ENTIRE DISH IS COOKED IN A SMALL PACKAGE OF PARCHMENT OR FOIL. WE USE OUR GLASS SERVING DISHES THEMSELVES AS THE "LITTLE PACKAGES." WE LIKE SNAPPER FOR THIS DISH BECAUSE IT HAS A GOOD FLAVOR AND WON'T FALL APART WHEN BAKED. EVEN PICKY EATERS WILL LIKE SOMETHING IN THIS ELEGANT BUT EASY ENTRÉE.

6	LEEKS,* WHITE AND LIGHT GREEN PARTS, THINLY SLICED
1	POUND CARROTS, SLICED
2	POUNDS RED POTATOES, VERY THINLY SLICED IN ROUNDS (SMALL POTATOES WORK BEST)
2	CLOVES GARLIC, MINCED
¼	CUP OLIVE OIL
¼	CUP MINCED FRESH THYME**
3	TEASPOONS SALT
1	TEASPOON PEPPER
4	POUNDS SNAPPER FILLETS
2	CUPS WHITE WINE
2	CUPS CHICKEN OR VEGETABLE BROTH
	SALT AND PEPPER TO TASTE
2	LEMONS, THINLY SLICED

GARNISH SUGGESTIONS

CHIVE STRANDS

FRESH THYME SPRIGS

Preheat oven to 425 degrees F.

Combine vegetables in a large bowl and gently toss with the oil, herbs, and seasonings. Divide this mixture equally among the co-op rectangular dishes.

Cut the fillets into individual serving pieces and lay them on top of the vegetables in each dish. Combine the wine and broth. Pour equal amounts of this liquid over the fish and vegetables in each dish.

Lightly salt and pepper fish and then fan lemon slices on top. Cover each dish tightly with aluminum foil and bake for 35 to 45 minutes. The potatoes should be barely tender.

*See Washing Leeks on page 76.

**Be free with your choice of herbs—tarragon, basil, marjoram, or parsley also work well in this dish. Diana uses what's fresh in the garden or the herb that fits her mood.

> I was really pleased and surprised by how good this was, since I'm not a huge fan of fish. The veggies are cooked to perfection and have a nice, light flavor.
>
> –Debbie on 20th Street

Serve with our Arugula and Goat Cheese Salad (see page 71).

Shrimp and Rice Bake with Gruyère and Thyme

SERVES 12

KIDS LOVE THIS SIMPLE, COMFORTABLE MEAL THAT COMES TOGETHER EASILY. THE PRONOUNCED FLAVOR OF FRESH THYME MAKES THE DISH MEMORABLE, THOUGH YOU CAN TRY IT WITH ENDLESS VARIATIONS, DEPENDING ON WHICH VEGETABLES AND HERBS YOU HAVE ON HAND.

3	CUPS RICE, UNCOOKED
¼	CUP BUTTER
1	LARGE ONION, DICED
1½	RED BELL PEPPERS, DICED
⅓	CUP WHITE WINE
4½	CUPS BROCCOLI FLORETS AND STALKS, SLICED IN COINS
1	CUP HALF-AND-HALF OR SOY CREAMER
12	OUNCES GRUYÈRE CHEESE, GRATED AND DIVIDED
1	OUNCE FRESH THYME, MINCED
1½	TEASPOONS PEPPER
2	TABLESPOONS OLIVE OIL
2	POUNDS SHRIMP, PEELED AND TAILS REMOVED

GARNISH SUGGESTIONS

FRESH THYME SPRIGS
ITALIAN PARSLEY SPRIGS
FRESH CHIVE FLOWERS

Prepare rice in a rice cooker or saucepan according to package directions or your favorite recipe.

Preheat oven to 350 degrees F.

Melt butter in a large soup pot over medium-low heat. Add onion and red peppers, and sauté until tender, about 6 minutes.

Add wine and broccoli to pot and sauté until bright green and barely tender. Transfer to a giant mixing bowl.

Add the cooked rice, half-and-half, two-thirds of the Gruyère, and the seasonings to the other ingredients in the large bowl.

Heat oil in a large nonstick pan over medium-high heat and sauté shrimp until opaque, 2 to 3 minutes. Gently fold the shrimp into the rice mixture. Divide the mixture among the round co-op dishes. Sprinkle the remaining cheese on top. Bake on the center rack of oven for 30 minutes, until centers are hot or cheese is melted.

> Piquant meets Peoria. Light and tasty but with the sturdiness of a casserole.
>
> –Gary on 10th Street

Serve with mixed fruit or a green salad, and send along some rustic bread to round out the meal.

Hunter Chicken with Artichoke Hearts

SERVES 12

TOMATOES, ORANGE ZEST, AND CAPERS COMBINE FOR A TART FRESH FLAVOR IN A SLURPABLE
SAUCE OVER LINGUINE. INCLUDE A SALAD ON THE SIDE AND YOU HAVE A CROWD-PLEASING MEAL
THAT SAYS "HOMEMADE."

¼ CUP CANOLA OIL
  SALT AND PEPPER TO TASTE
12 BONELESS SKINLESS CHICKEN
   BREAST HALVES OR THIGHS
3 ONIONS, SLICED
⅓ CUP GARLIC, MINCED
3 ORANGES, ZESTED
¾ CUP FRESH ORANGE JUICE
2 CUPS CHICKEN BROTH
28 OUNCES CANNED DICED
   TOMATOES*
42 OUNCES ARTICHOKE HEARTS,
   THAWED IF FROZEN
½ CUP CAPERS, DRAINED
2 TABLESPOONS FRESH THYME
  LEAVES, MINCED

GARNISH SUGGESTION

ITALIAN PARSLEY, CHOPPED

Heat oil in large sauté pan or large roasting pan over high heat. Salt and pepper the chicken and brown it on both sides. Remove chicken to a platter and cover.

Add onion and garlic to the pan and sauté over medium heat until onion is translucent.

Add orange zest, juice, broth, and tomatoes to onion and garlic, and simmer 15 minutes.

Return the chicken to the pan and add artichoke hearts, capers, and thyme. Continue simmering, uncovered, until chicken is cooked through and tender.

*See Special Ingredients for the Co-op Cook on page 155.

> This dish was absolutely **loved** by friends I gave it to and by everyone in my family, including the kids, who picked up their bowls and slurped the last bit.
>
> –Holly on Skylark Drive

Serve with Carrots and Snap Peas with Ginger Butter (see page 134).

Curry Chicken Stir-Fry with Rice Noodles

Serves 12

The aromas of curry and coconut milk and the sound of a hissing wok make your kitchen the place to be! A great way to split up your cooking time is to poach the chicken in advance. Improvise by changing the protein or the vegetables to suit your taste or the season.

21	OUNCES RICE NOODLES
¼	CUP SALT
2	POUNDS BROCCOLI, CUT INTO SMALL FLORETS, STEMS SLICED

Coconut Curry Sauce

3	CUPS COCONUT MILK, REGULAR, LIGHT, OR A MIXTURE
3	TABLESPOONS MILD-TO-HOT CURRY PASTE* (OR TO TASTE)
3	CUPS CHICKEN BROTH
1	LARGE ONION, DICED
½	CUP FRESH LIME JUICE*
2	HEADS GARLIC, MINCED
3	TABLESPOONS FISH SAUCE
3	TEASPOONS SUGAR

Putting It All Together

6	BONELESS SKINLESS CHICKEN BREAST HALVES, POACHED, COOLED AND SHREDDED OR DICED
45	OUNCES CANNED WHOLE STRAW MUSHROOMS, DRAINED
24	OUNCES CANNED SLICED BAMBOO SHOOTS, DRAINED

Garnish Suggestions

Limes, cut in wedges
Cilantro, chopped
Peanuts, crushed**

Soak noodles in lukewarm water for 15 to 30 minutes, until almost soft. Drain and set aside until needed.

Fill large pot with water and bring to a boil. Add salt and broccoli. Cook for 2 minutes. Strain and rinse with cold water to stop cooking. Set aside until needed.

Coconut Curry Sauce Make all the sauce at once, divide it, and then stir-fry each family's meal one at a time. The batch method won't crowd the wok and ensures the goodies are divided evenly.

In a soup pot over medium heat, warm the milk and curry paste, and stir until you smell the aroma of the curry. Add remaining ingredients to coconut milk and cook on high for 3 to 4 minutes. The sauce will thicken slightly. Remove from heat and set aside.

Putting It All Together Preheat oven to 200 degrees F. Add one household's portion of sauce to a wok or large skillet; over high heat, add one household's portion of rice noodles, broccoli, chicken, mushrooms, and bamboo shoots. Stir to combine and heat through, allowing noodles to absorb sauce. Turn off burner and arrange in first co-op dish; place in a warm oven. Now turn the burner back on and start the next batch. On the way out the door, garnish each dish.

*See Special Ingredients for the Co-op Cook on page 155.

**See Crushing Peanuts on page 63.

> I love the fresh flavor of lime in this curry. My sister liked the hint of coconut in the sauce, and I thought the bamboo shoots added a nice texture to the dish.
>
> –Lee on Riverview Drive

Chardonnay Chicken with Dried Fruit and Olives

SERVES 12

DRIED FRUIT AND OLIVES GIVE EVERYDAY CHICKEN A MEDITERRANEAN ACCENT IN THIS SILVER PALATE–INSPIRED DISH THAT WILL HAVE YOUR CO-OP CHEERING "MAGNIFICO!" THE KEY TO THIS DISH IS MARINATING IT OVERNIGHT. IF YOU'RE PRESSED FOR TIME THE NIGHT BEFORE, YOU CAN ROAST THE GARLIC THE NEXT DAY AND ADD IT TO THE CHICKEN BEFORE YOU PUT IT IN THE OVEN.

3	HEADS GARLIC, CLOVES SEPARATED FROM HEAD BUT NOT PEELED
3	CUPS CHARDONNAY
1½	CUPS OLIVE OIL
2	TABLESPOONS HERBES DE PROVENCE
1½	TEASPOONS DRIED LAVENDER FLOWERS
3	CUPS GREEN OLIVES, PITTED
1½	CUPS KALAMATA OLIVES, PITTED
4	CUPS DRIED WHOLE FRUIT, SUCH AS PEARS, APRICOTS, BLUEBERRIES
⅓	CUP CAPERS, DRAINED
3	BAY LEAVES, FRESH IF POSSIBLE
12	BONELESS SKINLESS CHICKEN BREAST HALVES
½	CUP BROWN SUGAR

Cook garlic in a nonstick pan on medium heat for 10 minutes to "dry roast" until soft; turn occasionally. Cool and then peel.

Combine remaining ingredients except brown sugar with garlic in a large Tupperware container, soup pot, or 2-gallon heavy-duty plastic bag and marinate in refrigerator overnight. Mix 1 or 2 times during the process so everything is evenly marinated.

Preheat oven to 350 degrees F.

Evenly distribute chicken and all of marinade and goodies into co-op rectangles. Sprinkle brown sugar over and bake for 50 minutes, uncovered. Check to make sure chicken is cooked through.

> **Lavender flowers and herbes de Provence add a light, aromatic note to the marinade.**
>
> –Debbie on 20th Street

Serve this dish with a rice or grain such as couscous, rice, or polenta to sop up all the wonderful juices. You can serve a green vegetable and crusty bread, if you prefer.

Rosemary Lime Chicken

SERVES 12

THIS IS A GREAT BASIC CHICKEN RECIPE THAT CAN BE USED IN MANY WAYS. USE IT AS A SIMPLE ENTRÉE OR TO TOP ANY SALAD. THE ROSEMARY OIL IS AN "EASY VERSION" OF ONE OF THOMAS KELLER'S METHODS, PRODUCING CHICKEN THAT'S EXTREMELY MOIST AND PERFECTLY INFUSED WITH ROSEMARY.

ROSEMARY OIL

6   CLOVES GARLIC, SEPARATED BUT NOT PEELED
2   TABLESPOONS SALT
1   OUNCE FRESH ROSEMARY LEAVES
1   CUP OLIVE OIL

CHICKEN

12   BONELESS SKINLESS CHICKEN BREAST HALVES
1   CUP FRESH LIME JUICE*

GARNISH SUGGESTION

LIMES, SLICED

ROSEMARY OIL   Cook garlic in nonstick pan on medium heat for 10 minutes to "dry roast" until soft; turn occasionally. Cool and then peel.

Bring a large pot of water to boil and add salt. Add rosemary to the pot and boil for 1 minute. Strain and run under cold water to stop the cooking and maintain color. Blot dry with a paper towel.

Place garlic and rosemary in blender with olive oil and blend for 2 to 3 minutes, until rosemary is well chopped and incorporated. The oil will start to turn green.

CHICKEN   Marinate chicken in Rosemary Oil for 1 hour up to overnight. Ziplock bags work great for marinating chicken. Pull chicken out of refrigerator 15 minutes before cooking to let oil come to room temperature. On the stovetop, bring a large roasting pan (or two sauté pans) to medium heat with a little of the marinade from the chicken to coat the bottom of the pan. When the pan is hot, add the chicken and cook for 5 minutes to brown. Flip and cook for 5 more minutes. Add the lime juice and let it coat the chicken. Check for doneness. If the chicken is not done, cover and reduce heat to medium-low until cooked through. Put chicken in serving dishes and spoon the small amount of remaining sauce over the chicken.

> The chicken was moist and bursting with flavor.
>
> –Judy on Wildbrooke

*See Special Ingredients for the Co-op Cook on page 155.

Serve with our Whole-Wheat Couscous with Orange Zest, Dried Cranberries, and Pumpkin Seeds (see page 144).

Layered Chicken Verde with Goat Cheese

SERVES 12

THE AVOCADO IN THIS SALSA VERDE GIVES THE LIGHT CREAMY SAUCE A LOVELY COLOR, AND THE CORN TORTILLAS, CHICKEN, AND CHEESE ADD UP TO A HEARTY MAIN DISH. SERVE WITH SLICED TOMATOES AND CHIPS AND SALSA ON THE SIDE, AND GARNISH WITH CILANTRO SPRIGS. IF YOU HAVE ANY EXTRA SAUCE, SEND IT ALONG IF YOU LIKE.

CHICKEN

3	TABLESPOONS OLIVE OIL
6	CLOVES GARLIC, MINCED
½	TEASPOON CHILE POWDER
6	BONELESS SKINLESS CHICKEN BREAST HALVES
½	CUP FRESH LIME JUICE
3	TABLESPOONS OLIVE OIL
2	MEDIUM ONIONS, DICED
3	RED BELL PEPPERS, DICED

HOMEMADE CREAMY SALSA VERDE

1	POUND TOMATILLOS,* HUSKED, RINSED, AND HALVED
6	CLOVES GARLIC, SEPARATED BUT NOT PEELED
14	OUNCES CANNED MILD GREEN CHILES
10	OUNCES GOAT CHEESE, CRUMBLED
8	OUNCES CREMA MEXICANA (THICK MEXICAN SOUR CREAM)
1	AVOCADO, SLICED
¾	CUP CILANTRO, STEMMED
1	LIME, ZESTED AND JUICED
1	TEASPOON GROUND WHOLE CUMIN
	SALT AND PEPPER TO TASTE

PUTTING IT ALL TOGETHER

5	CORN TORTILLAS PER FAMILY
3	CUPS MONTEREY JACK CHEESE, GRATED
	CILANTRO SPRIGS

CHICKEN In a large roasting pan or two sauté pans, heat oil over medium heat. Add garlic, chile powder, and chicken, and sauté for 5 minutes to brown. Flip and cook for 5 more minutes. Add the lime juice and allow it to coat the chicken. Check for doneness. If the chicken isn't done, cover and reduce heat to medium-low until cooked through. Cool the chicken a little, shred, and set aside in a large bowl. (If making ahead, refrigerate.)

In a large sauté pan, heat oil over medium-high and sauté onions for 5 minutes. Add peppers and sauté 5 more minutes. Take onions and peppers out of pan with slotted spoon and mix in with the chicken.

HOMEMADE CREAMY SALSA VERDE In a nonstick pan, dry-roast tomatillos and garlic over medium heat. You will need about 3 minutes per side for the tomatillos, 10 minutes total for the garlic. Roast until tomatillos are juicy and the garlic is soft, turning occasionally. Cool. Peel garlic. Add tomatillos and peeled garlic to blender with remaining ingredients and puree.

PUTTING IT ALL TOGETHER
Preheat oven to 350 degrees F.

Coat the bottom of each co-op round dish with some Creamy Salsa Verde. Place one tortilla on top of the sauce. Then layer Creamy Salsa Verde, chicken, cheese, and a tortilla in each dish. Continue with layers until you have used 5 tortillas in each family's meal, saving a little cheese for the end. Top final tortilla with Creamy Salsa Verde and remaining cheese. Cover with foil and bake for 30 minutes. Uncover and bake for 10 more minutes.

> A decadent weeknight treat! Rich, creamy, and slightly spicy, it's gourmet comfort food with a south-of-the border twist.
>
> –Debbie on 20th Street

---

*If you can't find fresh tomatillos, replace with canned. Skip the dry-roasting step, drain, and put directly in blender.

Southwestern Chicken Pot Pie

SERVES 12

POT PIES ARE PERFECT WINTER COMFORT FOOD. OUR VERSION FEATURES A SMOKY TOMATO-BASED SAUCE THAT'S EVOCATIVE OF MEXICAN MOLE SAUCE AND A RUSTIC CRUST WITH A HEARTY CORN FLAVOR. READ AHEAD TO SEE HOW TO MAKE THIS RECIPE IN STAGES AND ADJUST THE SPICE LEVEL ACCORDING TO THE NEEDS OF YOUR CO-OP.

Chicken

- 4 CUPS CHICKEN BROTH
- 1½ CUPS WATER
- 6 BONELESS SKINLESS CHICKEN BREAST HALVES

Filling

- 1½ TABLESPOONS OLIVE OIL
- ¾ POUND CHORIZO, CASINGS REMOVED
- 1 LARGE ONION, DICED
- 3 SMALL ZUCCHINIS, DICED
- 3 CLOVES GARLIC, MINCED
- 1½ JALAPEÑOS (OPTIONAL), MINCED
- 1 TEASPOON GROUND WHOLE CUMIN
- ½ TEASPOON ANCHO CHILE POWDER*
- ¾ CUP FLOUR
- 56 OUNCES CANNED FIRE-ROASTED TOMATOES,* DICED
- ¾ CUP CILANTRO LEAVES
- 1½ TABLESPOONS UNSWEETENED COCOA POWDER
- 1 TEASPOON CINNAMON

CHICKEN Heat broth and water in a soup pot over medium heat and poach chicken until done. This will take about 20 minutes. Remove from poaching liquid, cool, and dice into ½-inch bites.

FILLING Heat oil in large pan over medium-low heat and add chorizo. Sauté until browned, breaking up sausage into small pieces as it cooks.

Add ingredients from onions through chile powder to chorizo and cook for 10 minutes, stirring occasionally as needed.

Add flour to chorizo-onion mixture and cook for 5 minutes, stirring constantly.

Puree remaining ingredients in a blender (in batches if needed). Add to onion mixture and cook on low for 30 minutes to develop flavors and thicken. Take off heat. This filling may be refrigerated overnight if desired.

> The aroma of this meal as it cooks is fantastic.
>
> –Rejane on 11th Street

Serve with Avocado and Grapefruit Salad with Chile Maple Pecans (see page 61).

Rustic Corn Crust

1⅓ CUPS WHOLE-WHEAT PASTRY
     FLOUR
¾   CUP CORNMEAL, FINELY
     GROUND**
2   TEASPOONS BAKING POWDER
½   TEASPOON SALT
     DASH CINNAMON
8   OUNCES CREAM CHEESE, CUBED
8   TABLESPOONS BUTTER, SLICED

Putting It All Together

30   OUNCES CANNED BLACK BEANS,
     RINSED AND DRAINED
20   OUNCES FROZEN CORN, THAWED
14   OUNCES CANNED DICED GREEN
     CHILES
1   EGG
     DASH SALT

Garnish Suggestions
   (PACKAGE SEPARATELY)

     SOUR CREAM, ½ CUP PER FAMILY
     SALSA, 1 CUP PER FAMILY

RUSTIC CORN CRUST Place dry ingredients in food processor and pulse to combine ingredients.

Add cream cheese and butter to food processor and process until combined. Divide into 3 or 4 portions, and roll out on a floured surface (with floured rolling pin) into discs to cover the dishes you are using (7½-inch discs for co-op rounds). Cover in plastic and refrigerate until needed.

PUTTING IT ALL TOGETHER Preheat oven to 375 degrees F.

Mix beans, corn, and chiles into pot pie mixture and divide into co-op rounds. Place crust on top of each round. Mix egg with salt and "paint" on crust with pastry brush. Make a few slits in the crust to let steam escape. Bake for 40 to 50 minutes; crust should be golden brown.

*See Special Ingredients for the Co-op Cook on page 155.

**Cornmeal: If you do not use finely ground cornmeal for this crust, you will find the crust a bit too gritty. Look for it in a box in the bulk section or on the baking aisle. Polenta will not work well, as it is a coarsely ground cornmeal.

Shepherd's Pie with Curried Spinach

SERVES 12

HERE'S A FUN TWIST ON THE TRADITIONAL SHEPHERD'S PIE MADE WITH CHICKEN SAUSAGE INSTEAD OF LAMB. YOU CAN MAKE THE POTATOES AHEAD, OR EVEN ASSEMBLE THE WHOLE DISH THE NIGHT BEFORE, AND THEN COOL, COVER, AND REFRIGERATE UNTIL READY TO BAKE. IT'S VERY HEARTY AND PORTION SIZES ARE LARGE, SO FEEL FREE TO SERVE ONLY THIS FOR DINNER.

CHICKEN LAYER

1½ TABLESPOONS OLIVE OIL

3 LEEKS,* WHITE AND LIGHT GREEN PARTS, DICED

1 SMALL ONION, DICED

12 FULLY COOKED SAUSAGES, SLICED**

3 STALKS CELERY, DICED

6 CLOVES GARLIC, MINCED

¾ CUP FLOUR

1½ TABLESPOONS BUTTER

1½ CUPS WHITE WINE

3 GREEN APPLES, DICED

POTATOES

6 POUNDS RUSSET AND SWEET POTATOES (CHOOSE AMOUNTS OF EACH), PEELED AND CUT IN 2-INCH PIECES

2 TABLESPOONS SALT

6 TABLESPOONS SOUR CREAM

3 OUNCES GOAT CHEESE

¼ CUP OLIVE OIL

3 TABLESPOONS BUTTER

1½ TABLESPOONS MAPLE SYRUP

SALT AND PEPPER TO TASTE

(INGREDIENTS CONTINUED)

For this meal, 12 portions will fill 3 rectangle dishes or 4 rounds. Spray co-op dishes with cooking spray and set aside.

CHICKEN LAYER Heat oil in large saucepan over medium-low heat, add leeks and onion, and cook for 5 to 10 minutes, until soft.

Add sausage, celery, and garlic to leeks and onions. Cook for 5 minutes, stirring occasionally.

Add flour and butter to sausage mixture, stirring constantly for 5 minutes. Add wine and continue to cook, stirring for 2 more minutes. Turn off heat, add apples, stirring to combine, and transfer evenly into co-op dishes.

POTATOES Bring large pot of water to boil. Add the potatoes and salt, and boil until tender, about 20 to 25 minutes. Drain. Return to same pot with heat off.

Mix remaining ingredients into potatoes as you mash them. Set aside until ready to assemble. Refrigerate if making ahead of time.

> Humble Shepherd's Pie reaches a whole new level. You'll have to hold yourself back from scurrying away with the remaining casserole and one big spoon.
>
> Debbie on 20th Street

Continued on next page.

SPINACH LAYER

1½   TABLESPOONS OLIVE OIL
1½   TABLESPOONS CURRY PASTE***
2   CUPS MILK
50   OUNCES FROZEN CHOPPED
      SPINACH, THAWED AND DRAINED
6   OUNCES GOAT CHEESE,
      CRUMBLED
      DASH SALT

TO FINISH

3   TABLESPOONS BUTTER,
      THINLY SLICED

SPINACH LAYER Preheat oven to 350 degrees F.

Heat oil and curry paste in large pot for 3 minutes, stirring occasionally until fragrant. Add milk, stir, and bring to boil. Add spinach and stir once or twice until spinach is broken apart. Cover, lower heat to medium-low, and cook for 5 minutes.

Add cheese and salt to spinach and stir until cheese melts. Remove from heat and spread over chicken sausage layer.

TO FINISH Layer potatoes over spinach and dot with slivers of butter. Bake for 45 to 50 minutes, until heated through and potatoes have started to brown. (If you assembled the Shepherd's Pies in advance, pull them from the refrigerator while the oven is preheating to 350 degrees F; pies will take about 60 minutes to cook.)

*See Washing Leeks on page 76.

**We chose chicken and apple sausage to complement the apples in this recipe. Feel free to try other favorites as well. Aidells and Amy's make sausages we highly recommend. Check out a farmers market or ask your own Sausage Lady for some great local sausages.

***See Special Ingredients for the Co-op Cook on page 155.

Sausage with Baked Rosemary Polenta and Grilled Vegetables

SERVES 12

HERE WE'VE DISCOVERED A SUPER SIMPLE TECHNIQUE FOR MAKING POLENTA—NO CONTINUOUS STIRRING, JUST BAKE IN THE ROUND CO-OP DISHES. CHICKEN BROTH MAKES THE POLENTA REFRESHINGLY TANGY—FOR A MORE DELICATE FLAVOR, TRY SOME MILK IN PLACE OF THE BROTH. BROWNING A FLAVORFUL, PRECOOKED SAUSAGE MAKES THE MEAT PREPARATION IN THIS DISH QUICK AND EASY, LEAVING PLENTY OF TIME TO GRILL THE VEGETABLES.

BAKED ROSEMARY POLENTA

- 1 CUP CORNMEAL PER FAMILY
- 4 CUPS CHICKEN BROTH PER FAMILY
- 1 TEASPOON SALT PER FAMILY
- 1 TEASPOON FRESH ROSEMARY LEAVES, CHOPPED, PER FAMILY
- ¼ CUP HALF-AND-HALF OR SOY CREAMER PER FAMILY
- ½ CUP PARMESAN, GRATED (OR HALF GOUDA IF USING SAUSAGES WITH GOUDA) PER FAMILY

SAUSAGE AND GRILLED VEGETABLES

- 4 RED BELL PEPPERS, DICED INTO 1½-INCH PIECES
- 4 SMALL ZUCCHINI, SLICED
- 2 POUNDS ASPARAGUS, CUT ON BIAS IN 1½-INCH SLICES
- 1 SMALL RED ONION, CUT INTO RINGS
- 3 TABLESPOONS OLIVE OIL SALT AND PEPPER TO TASTE
- 3 POUNDS SAUSAGE (FULLY COOKED)*, SLICED ON THE BIAS
- 3 TABLESPOONS OLIVE OIL
- ¼ CUP BALSAMIC VINEGAR

BAKED ROSEMARY POLENTA Preheat oven to 375 degrees F.

Place 1 cup of cornmeal, 4 cups of stock, and 1 teaspoon of salt into each of the round containers. Stir and place in oven. Rotate dishes and stir halfway through cooking. Cook for 50 to 60 minutes, or until thickened. Meanwhile, start preparing the rest of the meal.

When polenta has thickened, remove from oven and stir 1 teaspoon rosemary, ¼ cup half-and-half, and ½ cup grated Parmesan into each round.

SAUSAGE AND GRILLED VEGETABLES Preheat grill on high heat, or plan to cook in 1 or 2 grill pans on a stovetop over medium heat.

Put all vegetables into a large bowl and toss with olive oil, salt, and pepper. Add vegetables to a grill basket or grill pans, and stir every 5 minutes until everything is cooked, 15 to 20 minutes. The vegetables should be a little charred but still be al dente. Alternately, vegetables may be sautéed on the stove.

Sauté sliced sausage in olive oil in large sauté pan (or 2 medium pans) until heated through. You can also grill them whole and then slice.

Toss vegetables with vinegar and divide into rectangular co-op dishes. Portion sausage over vegetables and deliver.

> This is the quintessential co-op dish! The combination of creamy polenta, colorful stir-fried vegetables, and beautifully browned sausage impressed even my eight- and eleven-year-old sons.
>
> –Janet on Parkside Drive

*A great sausage to use is Amy's Apple and Gouda Cheese Chicken Sausage.

Spinach, Lavender, and Goat Cheese Strata

SERVES 12

THE LAVENDER IN THIS DISH LETS US PRETEND WE'RE ON VACATION IN THE SOUTH OF FRANCE. STRATAS ARE WONDERFUL FOR CO-OP COOKING BECAUSE YOU CAN ASSEMBLE THEM AHEAD OF TIME AND ALLOW THE BREAD TO SOAK UP THE CUSTARD.

SPINACH LAYER

3	POUNDS FRESH SPINACH, LARGE STEMS REMOVED, CHOPPED
1	TEASPOON OLIVE OIL
1	LARGE ONION, DICED
4	CLOVES GARLIC, MINCED
	SALT AND PEPPER TO TASTE

CUSTARD

8	CUPS MILK (NOT NONFAT MILK)
12	EGGS
2	TABLESPOONS DIJON MUSTARD
2	TABLESPOONS GROUND FRESH LAVENDER FLOWERS
2	TABLESPOONS MINCED FRESH ROSEMARY LEAVES
½	TABLESPOON RED PEPPER FLAKES

STRATA

2	LONG FRENCH BREAD BAGUETTES (DAY OLD OR SLIGHTLY DRY)
12	OUNCES GOAT CHEESE, CRUMBLED
½	CUP CHOPPED FRESH CHIVES

GARNISH SUGGESTIONS
(CHOOSE TWO)

FRESH CHIVE STRANDS
FRESH CHIVE FLOWERS
FRESH LAVENDER FLOWERS
ITALIAN PARSLEY, CHOPPED

SPINACH LAYER Place spinach in a soup pot with a little water and cook, covered, until spinach wilts. Depending on the size of the pot, you may need to do this in two batches. Remove spinach to a colander to drain off any excess water.

In a dry soup pot, heat olive oil over medium heat. Add onions and cook until barely translucent, about 10 minutes. Add garlic and cook another minute, stirring. Combine wilted spinach with onions and season with salt and pepper. Remove from heat.

CUSTARD Whisk ingredients together in a large bowl until well blended.

STRATA Preheat oven to 350 degrees F.

Spray the bottom and sides of the rectangle co-op dishes with nonstick spray. Slice bread into ½-inch-thick slices. Place bread slices in a single layer to cover the bottom of the dishes. Next, distribute the spinach mixture evenly among the serving dishes. Top with the goat cheese. Sprinkle the chives over the cheese. Gently pour custard mixture over strata and let rest for 30 minutes or overnight if you wish. (Store in refrigerator if it sits longer than 30 minutes.)

Bake for 40 minutes, or until puffed and golden brown.

> A light and satisfying entree.
>
> –Debbie on 20th Street

Serve with our Fresh Green Beans with Orange Vinaigrette (see page 135).

Portobella Polenta with Wine and Figs

SERVES 12

MEATY PORTOBELLAS, RED WINE, AND FIGS COMBINE TO MAKE A VELVETY SAUCE FOR LAYERING WITH SOFT POLENTA. A SPRINKLING OF GORGONZOLA CHEESE ADDS RICHNESS. THE POLENTA IS PREPARED IN THE OVEN INSTEAD OF ON THE STOVETOP. THIS IS A REAL TIME-SAVER—NO CONTINUOUS STIRRING!

PORTOBELLA, WINE, AND FIG SAUCE

3	TABLESPOONS OLIVE OIL
2	LARGE ONIONS, SLICED
¼	CUP MINCED GARLIC
8	PORTOBELLA MUSHROOM CAPS, SLICED
1	POUND CREMINI MUSHROOMS, SLICED
2½	CUPS PORT WINE*
½	POUND DRIED MISSION FIGS, STEMMED AND HALVED LENGTHWISE
1	TEASPOON VANILLA EXTRACT
1	(1 X 2-INCH) STRIP ORANGE PEEL
3	TABLESPOONS MINCED FRESH ROSEMARY LEAVES
2	TEASPOONS BALSAMIC VINEGAR**

SALT AND PEPPER TO TASTE

POLENTA

2	TEASPOONS OLIVE OIL
12	CUPS MILK (OR WATER)
3	CUPS MEDIUM-COARSE POLENTA
1	TABLESPOON SALT
1	CUP GORGONZOLA CHEESE, CRUMBLED

PORTOBELLA, WINE, AND FIG SAUCE Heat the oil over medium-high heat in a large sauté pan until hot. Add onions and sauté until caramelized, about 10 to 15 minutes. Add garlic and sauté 2 more minutes. Add mushrooms and cook 10 minutes over high heat, stirring occasionally.

Simmer wine, figs, vanilla, and orange peel in a separate saucepan for 10 minutes until figs are plump. Discard orange peel. Add fig and wine mixture to the mushroom sauce and keep warm until polenta is cooked. (Sauce and mushrooms may be prepared up to this point ahead of time, refrigerated and then reheated while cooking polenta.)

Just before the polenta has finished cooking, add rosemary, vinegar, salt, and pepper to the sauce, and then remove sauce from heat.

POLENTA Preheat oven to 400 degrees F. Coat two 10- or 12-inch oven-proof skillets (or 9 x 13-inch baking dishes) with olive oil. The larger the skillet you choose, the shorter the cooking time will be.

Pour half of the milk, polenta, and salt into each skillet. Place both skillets into the oven and cook uncovered, 25 minutes, stirring once during cooking. Polenta is done when the milk is absorbed and the grains are thick but not too stiff.

Use polenta from one skillet to create a thin layer in the bottom of each co-op serving dish. Spoon half of Portobella, Wine, and Fig Sauce in an even layer on top of polenta. Top with the remaining polenta from the second skillet and the rest of the mushroom sauce. Sprinkle Gorgonzola on top of each dish.

*You may substitute dry red wine and ¼ cup brown sugar for port.

**See Special Ingredients for the Co-op Cook on page 155.

Serve with Carrots and Snap Peas with Ginger Butter or our Tangy Spinach Salad (see pages 134 and 67).

Black-Eyed Peas, Green Chiles, and Parmesan

SERVES 12

IF YOU'RE NEW TO BLACK-EYED PEAS, HERE'S A GREAT INTRODUCTION. THESE TENDER, SLIGHTLY CHEWY BEANS ARE BLENDED HERE WITH NUTTY BROWN RICE AND CREAMY SWISS CHEESE TO CREATE A TASTY SIDE DISH OR ENTRÉE. SOAKING BEANS MEANS PLANNING AHEAD OF TIME, BUT IT'S SO WORTH IT WHEN THEY'RE COOKED FROM SCRATCH IN BROTH AND SEASONINGS.

BLACK-EYED PEAS

- 4½ CUPS DRIED BLACK-EYED PEAS, WASHED AND SORTED
- 2 TABLESPOONS OLIVE OIL
- 2 ONIONS, DICED
- 3 CLOVES GARLIC, MINCED
- 4 CUPS CHICKEN OR VEGETABLE BROTH
- 5 CUPS WATER
- 2 BAY LEAVES
- 1 JALAPEÑO PEPPER, MINCED

RICE

- 3 CUPS LONG-GRAIN BROWN RICE
- 8 OUNCES EMMENTHALER OR SWISS CHEESE, GRATED
- 14 OUNCES CANNED DICED ROASTED GREEN CHILES
  SALT TO TASTE
  CANNED CHIPOTLE PEPPERS IN ADOBO SAUCE, PUREED (OPTIONAL), TO TASTE
- 1 CUP GRATED PARMESAN

GARNISH SUGGESTION

(CHOOSE ONE)

CILANTRO LEAVES, CHOPPED
ITALIAN PARSLEY, CHOPPED

BLACK-EYED PEAS Cover the peas with water in a large saucepan or soup pot and soak for 6 hours or overnight. Drain when ready to use.

In a soup pot, heat oil over medium heat and sauté onions and garlic until onions are translucent, about 10 minutes.

Add broth, water, bay leaves, jalapeño, and drained black-eyed peas to the onion mixture and bring to a boil. Reduce heat, cover, and simmer gently for 1 hour or until peas are barely tender. Drain off any excess liquid.

RICE While peas are cooking, prepare the rice according to package directions. This takes 45 to 60 minutes.

Preheat oven to 375 degrees F.

Combine cooked rice and peas in a large bowl while still warm. Add cheese, chiles, salt, and chipotle peppers (if you want to crank up the heat). Gently stir until ingredients are mixed evenly. Divide black-eyed pea mixture among the serving dishes.

Sprinkle Parmesan over each portion. Bake uncovered at 375 degrees F for 10 to 15 minutes until Parmesan is slightly golden brown. Serve hot or at room temperature.

> If you have any left over, try folding them into a tortilla with scrambled eggs.
>
> –John on 20th Street

Serve with our Mexican Salad with Corn, Mango, and Tomatoes (see page 65).

Tofu Triangles with Caramelized Onions and Smoked Paprika Red Peppers

SERVES 12

TOFU IS MARINATED IN OUR TANGY SPINACH SALAD DRESSING AND BROILED UNTIL BROWN. ONIONS AND PEPPERS COMPLEMENT THE DISH, WHICH CAN BE SERVED WITH ANY GRAIN OR VEGETABLE. ANDY AND DIANA ONCE USED THIS DISH IN A COOKING CLASS AND ARE STILL GETTING REQUESTS FOR THE RECIPE.

TANGY SPINACH SALAD DRESSING

- 1/3 CUP RED WINE VINEGAR
- 1/3 CUP DRY RED WINE
- 1/3 CUP HONEY
- 1/4 CUP SUGAR
- 1 CUP KETCHUP
- 1 TABLESPOON WORCESTERSHIRE SAUCE
- 2 TEASPOONS DIJON MUSTARD
- 2 TEASPOONS CURRY POWDER
- 2 TEASPOONS DRIED DILL WEED
- 4 CLOVES GARLIC, MINCED
- 1 CUP OLIVE OIL

TOFU AND VEGETABLES

- 4 POUNDS FIRM TOFU
- 2 TABLESPOONS OLIVE OIL
- 1 SWEET ONION, SLICED
- 2 ONIONS, SLICED
- 2 TABLESPOONS BALSAMIC VINEGAR*
- 1 TABLESPOON OLIVE OIL
- 3 RED BELL PEPPERS, JULIENNED
- 1 TEASPOON SMOKED PAPRIKA*

GARNISH SUGGESTION

(CHOOSE ONE)

ITALIAN PARSLEY, CHOPPED
FRESH CHIVES, CHOPPED

TANGY SPINACH SALAD DRESSING Whisk together everything in a large bowl. Cover and set aside at room temperature for 30 minutes or up to 2 hours to blend flavors. This marinade can be made ahead and refrigerated for up to 2 weeks.

TOFU AND VEGETABLES Preheat broiler.

Slice across each brick of tofu to create 3 large rectangular slabs approximately 1/2 inch thick. Lay the tofu slices on a clean cotton dishtowel. Cover the slices with another towel and place a heavy sheet pan on top of it all. Let the tofu drain like this for 15 minutes. Remove the sheet pan and towels. Spray two sheet pans with nonstick spray. Cut tofu rectangles diagonally to make 2 triangles from each slice. Dip each triangle into the marinade and place them close together on prepared sheet pans. Reserve remaining marinade.

Heat oil in a large sauté pan over medium heat and cook onions for 10 to 15 minutes, until just starting to become golden. Stir in the vinegar and remove from heat.

Heat oil over medium heat in separate sauté pan. Sauté peppers with paprika for about 10 minutes, or until peppers are very soft and browning slightly. Set them aside while you broil the tofu.

Broil tofu about 3 inches from the broiler heat until marinade is bubbly and tofu is golden brown on the top, 5 to 7 minutes. While tofu is broiling, warm remaining marinade in a saucepan on the stove.

Divide onions among serving dishes. Arrange the tofu triangles on the onions, fanning them to make a nice presentation. Spoon some of the reserved marinade over tofu. Top with the seasoned red peppers.

*See Special Ingredients for the Co-op Cook on page 155.

Create a complete meal by placing a generous layer of fresh spinach leaves in the bottom of the serving dish before adding onions, tofu, and peppers, or serve with our Wheat Berries with Roasted Red Peppers and Carrots (see page 149).

Zucchini, Sun-Dried Tomato, and Parmesan Tart

12 SERVINGS (3 TARTS)

THIS TART MAKES A LIGHT SUMMER MEAL WHETHER IT'S SERVED WARM OR AT ROOM TEMPERATURE. THE PUFF PASTRY CRUST STAYS CRISP AND DRY, AND SUN-DRIED TOMATOES ADD THEIR DISTINCT TART FLAVOR. IF YOU'VE NEVER USED PUFF PASTRY, YOU COULD GET HOOKED—IT'S A DELICIOUS GOURMET SHORTCUT AND IS EASY TO WORK WITH.

PASTRY CRUSTS

(MAY BE PREBAKED, COOLED, WRAPPED, AND KEPT AT ROOM TEMPERATURE UP TO TWO DAYS)

	PARCHMENT PAPER
2	BOXES FROZEN PUFF PASTRY, THAWED AS DIRECTED
	FLOUR FOR WORK SURFACE
1	EGG, BEATEN
6	OUNCES PARMESAN, GRATED

TART FILLING

2	POUNDS ZUCCHINI, GRATED
1	TABLESPOON SALT
1	TABLESPOON OLIVE OIL
2	LARGE RED ONIONS, SLICED
8	OUNCES OIL-PACKED SUN-DRIED TOMATOES, DRAINED AND SLIVERED
	SALT TO TASTE

ASSEMBLING TART

6	EGGS
¼	CUP HALF-AND-HALF OR SOY CREAMER

PASTRY CRUSTS Preheat oven to 425 degrees F.

Line 3 sheet pans with parchment paper. You will be making one tart for each family. Carefully unfold 1 sheet of puff pastry on lightly floured cutting surface. Use the fold lines as a guide to cut this whole sheet into 3 narrow rectangles. Unfold another pastry sheet and place next to one of the narrow pieces on a sheet pan. Brush egg along one edge. Overlap the long edge of the smaller piece and press the edges together gently. Brush egg all along edges of this now-larger sheet of pastry. Create a crust by gently folding over about $1/2$ inch of the outside edge, pressing gently so it will stick. Repeat with the remaining pastry sheets to make 3 crusts.

Use a fork to poke many uniform holes in the tart shells. Spread the cheese evenly over the crust bottoms. Bake for 10 minutes at 425 degrees F and then reduce heat to 350 degrees F and bake another 10 minutes until crust is golden brown, rotating sheet pans as necessary. If crust puffs up too much during baking, use a fork to prick a few more holes in the dough to release steam. Remove crusts and increase oven temperature to 400 degrees F.

TART FILLING Combine zucchini and salt, and drain in a colander for 15 minutes. Use a salad spinner to gently remove extra moisture from zucchini.

Heat oil in a medium sauté pan over medium-high heat. Add onions and cook, stirring occasionally, until onions caramelize, about 10 to 15 minutes. Remove from heat and stir in tomatoes. Salt to taste. Spread onion mixture over the bottom of tart crusts. Distribute zucchini evenly on top.

ASSEMBLING TART Beat together eggs and half-and-half, and spoon over vegetables. Use a ladle to divide custard evenly between each tart. Bake at 400 degrees F for 20 minutes, or until filling is set. Let the tarts cool 5 minutes. Deliver the tarts whole on their sheet pans, or cut into squares and layer slices between wax paper in the serving dishes.

Serve with our Pesto Chickpeas and Mixed Greens (see page 62).

Indian Curry with Tofu

SERVES 12

THE EXCITING FLAVORS IN THIS CLASSIC CURRY COME FROM THE TRADITIONAL INDIAN SPICES FENUGREEK, FRESH CURRY LEAVES, MUSTARD SEEDS, AND FRESH GINGER. IF YOU HAVE ACCESS TO AN INDIAN MARKET, THIS RECIPE WILL GIVE YOU A GOOD EXCUSE TO WANDER IN AND MAKE SOME DISCOVERIES. SERVE WITH BASMATI RICE, CHUTNEY, RAITA, AND WARM BUTTERED NAAN FOR AN AUTHENTIC AND DELICIOUS INDIAN MEAL.

½ CUP CANOLA OIL

2 TABLESPOONS MUSTARD SEEDS

2 TABLESPOONS FENUGREEK SEEDS

3–5 JALAPEÑO PEPPERS, SLICED IN ROUNDS

¼ CUP FRESH GINGER,* MINCED

3 HANDFULS FRESH CURRY LEAVES,** TORN INTO SMALL PIECES

3 LARGE ONIONS, DICED

1 POUND WHITE OR RED POTATOES, PEELED AND DICED

2 POUNDS ZUCCHINI SQUASH, SLICED IN ROUNDS***

9 ROMA TOMATOES, DICED

28 OUNCES CANNED COCONUT MILK

16 OUNCES FIRM TOFU, CUT IN ½-INCH CUBES

1 TABLESPOON CHILE POWDER

1 TABLESPOON TURMERIC

SALT TO TASTE

1 POUND FRESH SPINACH LEAVES, ROUGHLY CHOPPED

GARNISH SUGGESTIONS

CILANTRO LEAVES
MANGO CHUTNEY
CUCUMBER RAITA****

Heat oil in a large soup pot over medium heat. When hot, add mustard seeds. After they pop, add fenugreek, jalapeño, ginger, and curry leaves. Stir and fry 3 minutes.

Add onions and potatoes to spices and cook over medium heat until onions are beginning to brown. Add ¼ cup of water to the pot. Cover and continue cooking until potatoes are nearly tender.

Add ingredients from zucchini through turmeric to onion/potato mixture. Simmer 10 minutes, until vegetables are cooked through and sauce begins to thicken. Salt to taste.

Stir spinach into curry and cook another minute just to wilt the spinach.

*See Special Ingredients for the Co-op Cook on page 155.

**Fresh curry leaves are very sturdy (like lime leaves) and add a complex flavor to this dish. They aren't always on display in Indian markets—sometimes we have to ask for them to be brought out of a cooler in the back. If you can't locate them, substitute 1 tablespoon curry powder.

***Other vegetables we like to use are eggplant, green beans, and broccoli or cauliflower florets. You may need to adjust the cooking time a bit.

****Raita is a cooling yogurt-based condiment for spicy curries that's easy to make: Mix together 2 cups of plain yogurt with 1 peeled and finely chopped cucumber. Add a little fresh mint and salt to taste. Serve separately.

> I'm having the leftover Indian Curry for lunch today, and people keep stopping in the hallway and asking, "What smells so wonderful?" and "That's making me *really* hungry."
>
> –Debbie on 20th Street

Swiss Chard Spanakopita with Feta

SERVES 12

THE FLAKY PHYLLO CRUST ADDS UNEXPECTED DECADENCE TO AN EXTREMELY HEALTHY WEEKNIGHT DISH.
YOU'LL FEEL GREAT MAKING THIS FOR YOUR GROUP—SWISS CHARD HAS IT ALL: IRON AND VITAMINS A, C, AND
K. IT CONTRIBUTES TO BONE HEALTH, IS AN ANTIOXIDANT, AND IS HIGH IN FIBER. THIS SPANAKOPITA IS LIGHT
BUT VERY SATISFYING—A TREAT FOR LUNCH THE NEXT DAY.

SWISS CHARD FILLING

3   BUNCHES SWISS CHARD LEAVES,
    CUT IN STRIPS (RESERVE SWISS
    CHARD STEMS)
2   TABLESPOONS OLIVE OIL
2   ONIONS, DICED
2   CUPS SWISS CHARD STEMS, DICED
7   CLOVES GARLIC, MINCED
10 OUNCES FETA CHEESE, CRUMBLED
3   EGGS, BEATEN
    SALT AND PEPPER TO TASTE

PHYLLO

2   TABLESPOONS BUTTER, MELTED
2   TABLESPOONS OLIVE OIL
1   PACKAGE FROZEN PHYLLO DOUGH
    (REFRIGERATE OVERNIGHT AND
    THEN BRING TO ROOM TEMPERA-
    TURE BEFORE USING)
¼   CUP PINE NUTS, TOASTED

SWISS CHARD FILLING Fill a soup pot with $1\frac{1}{2}$ quarts water. Cook chard leaves, covered, over medium heat until they are wilted and the small red ribs are tender. Chard will cook down by about 50 percent. Rinse in cold water to stop the cooking process and drain in a colander. Press excess moisture out of chard leaves with hands. Transfer chard to a large bowl. If the soup pot is not big enough, it is fine to cook it in two batches.

Heat oil over medium heat in sauté pan. Add onions and chard stems, and sauté until they are translucent, about 10 minutes. Add garlic and continue to cook for 2 minutes. Add onion mixture to chard leaves in bowl. Stir feta, eggs, salt, and pepper into chard-and-onion mixture.

PHYLLO Preheat oven to 375 degrees F.

Combine butter with olive oil. Use a pastry brush to apply butter and oil mixture to bottom of baking dishes. You will continue to use the pastry brush to apply the "butter" to the phyllo as needed. Unfold phyllo on the counter and cover with a piece of plastic wrap and a clean, moist dishcloth.

If you're in a hurry, stop right now and take a deep breath and maybe a sip of wine. Phyllo does not respond well to stress vibes. It does respond well to moisture, so keep the stack of phyllo dough covered with the damp cloth. It will be much easier to wrangle into the dish.

Now fold one sheet of phyllo pastry in half and lay it in the serving dish. Brush with butter. Layer second folded sheet and brush with butter. Repeat for the rest of the serving dishes. Spread the chard mixture evenly onto the phyllo in each dish. Sprinkle pine nuts on top of the chard.

Layer 2 more folded sheets of phyllo on each spanakopita, brushing the top of each sheet with butter. Bake for 45 to 50 minutes, or until top is browned.

Serve with our Roasted Tomatoes Stuffed with Goat Cheese and Sage (see page 137) in the summer and
Curried Carrot Soup with Sweet Potatoes (see page 80) in the fall or winter.

Roasted Eggplant and Tomato Lasagna

SERVES 12

FRESH BASIL AND FIRE-ROASTED TOMATOES ADD UNIQUE FLAVOR TO THIS VEGETARIAN LASAGNA.
TOFU IS THE SECRET INGREDIENT THAT ADDS EXTRA CREAMINESS AND PROTEIN, AND NO ONE WILL EVER GUESS.
COMBINE THIS SAUCE WITH OUR MEATLOAF RECIPE TO GET GOURMET SPAGHETTI AND MEATBALLS.

ROASTED TOMATO SAUCE

3	TABLESPOONS OLIVE OIL
1	TABLESPOON DRIED OREGANO
2	TABLESPOONS DRIED BASIL
½	TABLESPOON RED PEPPER FLAKES
1	TEASPOON FENNEL SEED, GROUND
2	LARGE ONIONS, DICED
6	CLOVES GARLIC, MINCED
2	RED BELL PEPPERS, DICED
½	CUP DRY RED WINE
½	CUP WATER
28	OUNCES CANNED DICED TOMATOES, FIRE-ROASTED*
6	OUNCES CANNED TOMATO PASTE
28	OUNCES CANNED TOMATO SAUCE*

LASAGNA

2	LARGE EGGPLANTS, SLICED IN THIN ROUNDS
¼	CUP OLIVE OIL
	SALT AND PEPPER TO TASTE
1	OUNCE FRESH BASIL LEAVES, CHOPPED
8	OUNCES RICOTTA CHEESE
14	OUNCES FIRM TOFU
	SALT TO TASTE
1	POUND LASAGNA NOODLES, COOKED

GARNISH SUGGESTION

FRESH BASIL LEAVES, CHOPPED

ROASTED TOMATO SAUCE Heat oil in a soup pot over medium heat. Sprinkle in herbs and cook, stirring, for 30 seconds, until herbs become aromatic. Add onions and garlic, and sauté until translucent, about 10 minutes.

Add remaining ingredients to onion and herb mixture and simmer over medium-low heat, covered, for 30 to 45 minutes. (May be made ahead and reheated before serving.)

LASAGNA Preheat oven to 425 degrees F.

On 2 or 3 sheet pans place sliced eggplant. Brush both sides of eggplant lightly with olive oil and season with salt and pepper. Bake for 10 minutes, until just cooked through and browning. Remove from oven and set aside. Lower oven heat to 350 degrees F.

Blend basil, ricotta, tofu, and salt in food processor.

Smear a thin layer of sauce on the bottom of the co-op dishes. Then assemble the lasagna as follows: noodles, cheese mixture, eggplant slices, and sauce. Repeat 2 more times, ending with sauce. (If you are running low on eggplant or sauce, it is fine to repeat only one time.) Cover and bake for 35 minutes.

*See Special Ingredients for the Co-op Cook on page 155.

> A fast and easy lasagna with sauce made from scratch. I love that.
>
> –Holly on Skylark Drive

Serve with our Arugula and Goat Cheese Salad or our Caesar Salad (see pages 71 and 68).

New Orleans Sandwich in the Round

SERVES 12 (3 FAMILY-SIZE SANDWICHES)

ANYONE WHO'S VISITED NEW ORLEANS WILL RECOGNIZE THIS INSPIRED COUSIN OF THE MUFFALETTA, THE BIG EASY'S SIGNATURE SANDWICH. THE UNIQUE HOMEMADE RELISH IS A MIX OF DICED BLACK AND GREEN OLIVES, PICKLED ASPARAGUS, AND FRESH CAULIFLOWER TO ADD AN UNEXPECTED CRUNCH. THE KEY TO ANY KILLER SANDWICH IS FINDING HIGH-QUALITY INGREDIENTS. WE LOVE BOAR'S HEAD MEATS AND CHEESES, AVAILABLE AT OUR LOCAL DELI.

OLIVE AND PICKLED VEGETABLE RELISH

¾ CUP OLIVE OIL

1½ TABLESPOONS FRESH LEMON JUICE

1½ TABLESPOONS DIJON MUSTARD

1 TEASPOON MINCED GARLIC
PEPPER TO TASTE

7 OUNCES KALAMATA OLIVES, PITTED AND DICED SMALL

7 OUNCES SPANISH GREEN OLIVES WITH PIMIENTOS, DICED SMALL

12 OUNCES PICKLED ASPARAGUS SPEARS, DRAINED AND DICED SMALL

6 OUNCES CAULIFLOWER FLORETS, DICED SMALL

¾ OUNCE FRESH BASIL LEAVES, CHOPPED

SANDWICHES

3 ROUND ARTISAN LOAVES OF BREAD, SLICED IN HALF LENGTHWISE

¾ POUND HAM, THINLY SLICED

⅓ POUND SALAMI, THINLY SLICED

⅓ POUND COPPA SALAMI, SWEET OR SPICY, THINLY SLICED

1½ POUNDS HAVARTI, THINLY SLICED

3 LARGE TOMATOES, SLICED

1 HEAD ROMAINE, RINSED AND SEPARATED

OLIVE AND PICKLED VEGETABLE RELISH Mix oil, juice, mustard, garlic, and pepper together in a medium bowl.

Add remaining ingredients to olive oil dressing, toss, and set aside until needed (or make ahead and refrigerate).

SANDWICHES Preheat oven to 400 degrees F if you would like to serve sandwich warm.

Tear out bread from the inside of each half round, leaving a one-inch crust on all sides. This will leave you room for Olive and Pickled Vegetable Relish, meats, and cheeses without making the sandwich too crazy big to eat. (Save the torn pieces of bread for a strata or bread salad, or pulse in the food processor to make bread crumbs. Freeze to keep.)

Divide and spread relish on bottom halves of bread. Layer meats and cheese, ending with tomato. Top sandwich and wrap completely in foil. Bake for 30 minutes. Deliver in foil and allow families to cut in quarters or as desired. Package lettuce separately to add just before slicing. You can also serve this sandwich cold; in this case, add the lettuce on top of the tomatoes before you wrap it all up.

> The olive relish really adds zing to this sandwich. Served on a nice loaf of bread, it turns an ordinary deli sandwich into a meal with flare.
>
> –Paul on East State Street

Serve with your favorite tomato soup or our Wild Rice and Chickpea Salad (see page 147).

Roast Beef Sandwich with Goat Cheese Spread and Black Olive Tapenade

SERVES 12

To create the best sandwich you can bite into, splurge on high-quality roast beef sliced thick from your favorite deli. Flaky ciabatta wraps around flavorful roast beef layered with creamy cheeses and a snappy tapenade. Enjoy with a glass of Pinot Noir and someone who loves red meat.

TAPENADE

- 9 OUNCES KALAMATA OLIVES, DRAINED AND PITTED
- 3 ROASTED RED PEPPERS, FROM A JAR OR HOMEMADE
- 2 TABLESPOONS CAPERS
- 2 TABLESPOONS BALSAMIC VINEGAR*

GOAT CHEESE SPREAD

- 10 OUNCES GOAT CHEESE
- 4 OUNCES CREAM CHEESE, "SPREADABLE" SUCH AS NANCY'S
- 4 OUNCES SOUR CREAM
- 2 TABLESPOONS OLIVE OIL
- ½ CUP FINELY GRATED ASIAGO CHEESE
  PEPPER TO TASTE

SANDWICHES

- 3 LOAVES CIABATTA BREAD, SLICED IN HALF LENGTHWISE
- 3¾ POUNDS ROAST BEEF, THICKLY SLICED
- 6 HANDFULS BUTTER LETTUCE, RINSED AND SEPARATED

TAPENADE Pulse all ingredients in food processor until finely chopped.

GOAT CHEESE SPREAD Mix all ingredients by hand or with a food processor until well combined.

SANDWICHES Open up loaves and spread goat cheese mixture on the bottom. Top with butter lettuce and then roast beef. Spread the tapenade on the top layer of bread. Put the sandwich together and wrap well. Deliver the giant sandwich in one piece and then let the families cut to size, or you may cut in half if it's easier.

This sandwich holds up well when assembled. You may make it hours ahead and refrigerate. It's one of many of our dishes that work great for a potluck. Before the party (or at the party), slice thin sandwiches and use fancy toothpicks to hold them together. Arrange on a platter with a little lettuce and dress up the plate with a few whole kalamata olives.

*See Special Ingredients for the Co-op Cook on page 155.

This sandwich is the perfect co-op choice when it's too hot to cook but you hunger for a substantial meal.

—Debbie on 20th Street

Serve with our Curried Carrot Soup (see page 80) or with roasted asparagus.

Cobb Sandwich on Fresh Bakery Bread

SERVES 12

ALEX'S NEIGHBOR GLORIA ONCE WHIPPED UP A BATCH OF THESE OUTRAGEOUS SANDWICHES AND BROUGHT THEM OVER ON A PLATE. PERFECTLY COOKED BACON, HARD-BOILED EGGS, AND RIPE AVOCADOES MAKE THIS SANDWICH A GUILTY PLEASURE. ADD TANGY BLUE CHEESE DRESSING AND SEND YOUR GROUP INTO A PROTEIN-INDUCED STATE OF ECSTASY.

PARCHMENT OR WAX PAPER

4 SQUARE LOAVES FRESH BAKERY BREAD,* SLICED BY HAND

2 POUNDS NATURAL CHICKEN, DELI-SLICED (SUCH AS BOARS HEAD)

2 POUNDS BACON, THICK-SLICED AND COOKED

6 SMALL AVOCADOES, SLICED

12 EGGS, MEDIUM TO JUMBO, HARD BOILED**

24 OUNCES BLUE CHEESE DRESSING (FROM REFRIGERATOR CASE)

24 FESTIVE SANDWICH TOOTHPICKS

Make four sandwiches at a time: Lay out an ample sheet of parchment or wax paper for each sandwich, place two slices of bread on each sheet, and start building. For each sandwich, layer 2 slices of chicken, 2 to 3 slices of bacon, 4 to 5 avocado slices (half an avocado), and 1 sliced hard-boiled egg on one slice of bread.

Spread the remaining slices of bread with a generous glob of blue cheese dressing. Top each sandwich and press down—the dressing should help glue it all in place.

Wrap parchment or wax paper tightly up and around the sandwich. With a sharp knife, cut diagonally through paper and sandwich. Insert a festive pick into each half. If desired, write messages on the wrappers or label with each person's name. Stack inside rectangular dishes. Now you are ready to make the next batch of four. Continue until you have made one for everyone in the co-op.

*If you are a baker, this sandwich offers an excellent showcase for home-baked bread.

**Perfect Hard-Boiled Eggs: Place eggs in a large pot and fill with water to just cover eggs. Quickly bring to a boil and then remove from heat. Cover and rest for exactly eighteen minutes. Drain and cool in ice water for 5 to 10 minutes. Drain immediately and use or refrigerate. This method produces beautiful bright-yellow yolks.

> These are a hit. My kids love the blue cheese dressing and colored tooth-picks. The wax paper wraps are perfect. Definitely a keeper!
>
> —Jenifer on 20th Street

Serve with our Caesar Salad, Roasted Asparagus Soup with Lemon (see pages 68 and 76), or a simple fruit salad.

Grilled Salmon Sandwich with Lemon Dill Dressing

SERVES 12

THE GRILLED SALMON IN THESE APPEALING SANDWICHES CAN BE SERVED COLD OR AT ROOM TEMPERATURE, MAKING THIS DISH TIME-FLEXIBLE. BLEND THE LEMON DILL DRESSING AND POACH THE EDIBLE LEMON WHEELS IN ADVANCE TO BUY YOURSELF MORE FREE TIME ON YOUR COOKING DAY. SERVE WITH A REFRESHING MIX OF CUT FRUIT.

LEMON DILL DRESSING

- ¾ CUP OLIVE OIL
- ¾ CUP PASTEURIZED EGG PRODUCT (SUCH AS EGG BEATERS)
- 1½ LEMONS, ZESTED (USE FOR SOME OF JUICE)
- ⅓ CUP FRESH LEMON JUICE
- 2 OUNCES FRESH DILL LEAVES
- 1 TABLESPOON DIJON MUSTARD
- 1 TEASPOON SALT
  PEPPER TO TASTE

LEMON WHEELS

- 3 LEMONS, SLICED VERY THINLY

SALMON

- LEMONS, SLICED IN WEDGES
- 4 POUNDS SALMON FILLETS, WITH SKIN ON (1 FILLET PER HOUSE-HOLD WORKS WELL)
  FRESH CHIVE STRANDS

PACKAGE SEPARATELY FOR DELIVERY

- 3 CUCUMBERS, SKIN PEELED IN STRIPES AND THINLY SLICED
- 6 HANDFULS MIXED GREENS
- 3 LOAVES CIABATTA, CUT INTO SANDWICH LENGTHS, SPLIT, AND INDIVIDUALLY WRAPPED

LEMON DILL DRESSING Place all ingredients in a blender or food processor and blend. Portion out in small containers and refrigerate. This dressing may be made 2 days ahead of time.

LEMON WHEELS Poach gently in water for 20 minutes to make the rinds tender enough to eat. Gently remove and let cool.

SALMON Spray nonstick spray on a paper towel and rub on grill. Preheat grill to high heat.

Squeeze a little lemon juice on each piece of salmon. Grill fillets skin side down on high heat for the first 8 to 9 minutes and then on medium for 5 minutes, until the thickest part just begins to flake. Peel skin off bottom, place fillets in co-op dishes, and garnish with chives. Place in refrigerator if not serving soon.

PACKAGE SEPARATELY FOR DELIVERY With this particular sandwich, we like to serve everything à la carte and let co-op members assemble it when they eat. The dressing is so good, you will want to let people know to put it on both sides of the bread.

Spice up this sandwich by swapping the Lemon Dill Dressing for our

Lemon Wasabi Sauce
1 cup mayonnaise
1 cup plain yogurt
3 tablespoons soy sauce
2 tablespoons lemon juice
2 tablespoons wasabi paste

Whisk together and chill.

Serve with our Spinach and Edamame Soup (see page 75) or a refreshing mix of cut fruit.

Chicken Pizza with Red Onions, Pineapple, and Sage

SERVES 12 (3 PIZZAS)

FRESH PINEAPPLE, RED ONION, ASIAGO, AND SAGE—THIS RECIPE OFFERS SOME UNEXPECTED TWISTS TO MAKE BARBECUE CHICKEN PIZZA A GREAT NEW EXPERIENCE. MARINATE THE CHICKEN AND PREPARE THE ROASTED RED PEPPER SAUCE THE NIGHT BEFORE, LEAVING LITTLE TO DO ON COOKING DAY BUT PUT THE PIZZAS TOGETHER. IF YOUR CO-CHEFS HAVE ROUND PIZZA PANS, BORROW THEM AHEAD OF TIME.

ROASTED RED PEPPER SAUCE

8	ROASTED RED PEPPERS, FROM A JAR OR HOMEMADE
1/4	CUP BALSAMIC VINEGAR
1 1/2	TABLESPOONS DIJON MUSTARD
1 1/2	TABLESPOONS OLIVE OIL
1	TEASPOON PEPPER

CHICKEN

3	POUNDS BONELESS SKINLESS CHICKEN BREAST HALVES, CUBED

PIZZAS

3	BALLS PREPARED DOUGH* CORNMEAL FOR THE WORK SURFACE
2	POUNDS FRESH MOZZARELLA, THINLY SLICED
2 1/2	CUPS DICED FRESH PINEAPPLE (1 PINEAPPLE SHOULD DO IT)
1/2	RED ONION, JULIENNED
3/4	CUP DICED RED BELL PEPPER
1/3	CUP GRATED ASIAGO CHEESE
3/4	OUNCE FRESH SAGE LEAVES, MINCED
1 1/2	TABLESPOONS OLIVE OIL

ROASTED RED PEPPER SAUCE Puree all ingredients in a blender. Simmer in a medium sauté pan for 8 to 10 minutes to make sauce thicker. Cool. Use 1/4 of the sauce to marinate the chicken and reserve the rest separately.

CHICKEN Marinate chicken in roasted red pepper sauce for 30 minutes to overnight. Sauté chicken in its marinade in a large sauté pan until chicken is cooked through.

PIZZAS Preheat oven to 425 degrees F. Remove dough from refrigerator and let it rest for 20 to 30 minutes at room temperature. This will allow it to expand a little before you roll it out so it doesn't keep shrinking on you. Sprinkle cornmeal on the working surface and on the pizza pans. Roll out each ball of dough into a circle (or rectangle if using a standard sheet pan) to match the size of the pizza pan and let rest for about 10 minutes. Then roll out again and place on the pan. Grab about 1/3 inch of dough from the edge of the pizza, bring forward and press to make the crust. Work all the way around.

Spread the reserved Roasted Red Pepper Sauce over the pizzas. Evenly space mozzarella over sauce and then layer remaining ingredients from pineapple to sage leaves.

> It's a fun unusual alternative, and we'll definitely make it again in the summer when we can use our own sage!
>
> —Lee on Riverview Drive

Drizzle oil on crusts of each pizza. Bake for 15 to 20 minutes, rotating pans as needed. Cover with foil and deliver. If your co-op families are not going to sit down to eat right away, you can deliver it unbaked—just let them know in advance to preheat oven to 425 degrees F.

*See Prepared Dough on page 131.

Creamy Pesto Pizza with Zucchini Ribbons

SERVES 12 (3 PIZZAS)

THIS DISH IS EASY TO MAKE AND PRETTY TO BEHOLD. THE RICOTTA CHEESE GIVES IT A DISTINCT CREAMY TEXTURE AND PESTO ADDS PIZZAZZ. ZUCCHINI RIBBONS ARE FANNED OUT ON TOP FOR A BEAUTIFUL SPOKE-LIKE PRESENTATION. OUR PESTO IS SIMPLE TO MAKE, BUT IF BASIL IS OUT OF SEASON, YOU CAN USE PREPARED PESTO FROM THE MARKET. IF EVERYONE IN YOUR CO-OP HAS A ROUND PIZZA PAN, BORROW THEM AHEAD OF TIME. HAVE FUN!

BASIL PESTO

4	OUNCES FRESH BASIL LEAVES
¾	CUP PINE NUTS, TOASTED
1½	CUPS GRATED PARMESAN OR ASIAGO
½	CUP OLIVE OIL

PIZZAS

3	BALLS PREPARED DOUGH* CORNMEAL FOR THE WORK SURFACE
1	CUP WHOLE-MILK RICOTTA CHEESE
3	SMALL ZUCCHINI, SLICED LENGTHWISE WITH VEGETABLE PEELER INTO RIBBONS
¾	CUP CHOPPED WALNUTS, TOASTED
⅓	CUP FINELY GRATED PARMESAN
2	TABLESPOONS OLIVE OIL RED PEPPER FLAKES (OPTIONAL)

GARNISH SUGGESTION

FRESH TOMATOES, CHOPPED

BASIL PESTO Place all pesto ingredients except olive oil in the food processor and pulse until roughly chopped. Then with motor running, drizzle olive oil in and process until incorporated. Set aside. Pesto may be made one day ahead and refrigerated. If it is made ahead, pour a small amount of olive oil on top of pesto to keep it fresh and green.

PIZZAS Preheat oven to 425 degrees F.

Remove dough from refrigerator and let rest for 20 to 30 minutes at room temperature. This will allow it to expand a little before you roll it out so it doesn't keep shrinking on you. Sprinkle cornmeal on the working surface and on the pizza pans. Roll out each ball of dough into a circle (or rectangle if using a standard sheet pan) to match the size of the pizza pan and let rest for about 10 minutes. Then roll out again and place on the pan. Grab about ⅓ inch of dough from the edge of the pizza, bring forward and press to make the crust. Work all the way around.

With the back of a spoon, spread ricotta evenly over pizzas, then layer pesto on top. Fan the zucchini ribbons in a circular pattern, covering most of the pizza, starting in the center like spokes of a wheel. (If using sheet pans, layer in overlapping stripes.) Sprinkle the walnuts and cheese over zucchini and drizzle a little olive oil on crust of pizza. If you want to spice it up, sprinkle red pepper flakes on top or put some in a small container for families to use as they like. Bake for 15 to 20 minutes, rotating pans as needed. Cover with foil and deliver. If your co-op families are not going to sit down to eat right away, you can deliver it unbaked—just let them know in advance to preheat oven to 425 degrees F.

*Prepared Dough: Supermarkets often carry prepared dough, but if you enjoy making your own dough and have time to do it, try substituting whole-wheat pastry flour for the all-purpose flour.

Edamame with Roasted Tomatoes and Bacon

SERVES 12

STEAMED EDAMAME PODS SPRINKLED WITH COARSE SALT ARE A BELOVED APPETIZER IN ASIAN RESTAURANTS. SHELLED EDAMAME (SOYBEANS) ARE AN EASY, VERSATILE INGREDIENT THAT ADDS A MILD NUTTY FLAVOR, BRIGHT GREEN COLOR, AND HEALTHY PROTEIN TO AN ARRAY OF DISHES. WE'VE KNOWN KIDS WHO WON'T EAT THEIR PEAS BUT WILL ABSOLUTELY CHOW DOWN ON EDAMAME. WHEN YOU ADD A LITTLE BACON, WHO COULD RESIST?

12	OUNCES BACON*
6	PINTS CHERRY OR PEAR TOMATOES, YELLOW OR RED
3	TABLESPOONS OLIVE OIL
	SALT TO TASTE
16	OUNCES FROZEN SHELLED EDAMAME, THAWED
2	TABLESPOONS BALSAMIC VINEGAR**
	PEPPER TO TASTE

GARNISH SUGGESTION

ITALIAN PARSLEY SPRIGS

Preheat oven to 400 degrees F.

Cook bacon in a skillet on medium-low until cooked to taste. Remove and drain on paper towels. When cooled, crumble or cut bacon into bite-size pieces.

Slice the tomatoes in half and toss with olive oil and salt. Spread tomatoes on a baking sheet and bake at 400 degrees F for 15 minutes.

Add edamame and roast for 5 more minutes.

Combine bacon with the vegetables. Add balsamic vinegar and pepper to taste. Divide among serving dishes.

*When you need less bacon than a full package, cook it all anyway. Crumble the extra bacon and store it in an airtight container in the freezer for use another time in a salad or garnish for a soup.

**See Special Ingredients for the Co-op Cook on page 155.

We love the color and crunch of the edamame, and when you add fresh tomatoes and crisp bacon, it's quite an exciting dish.

–Lee on Riverview Drive

Serve with our Pesto Pasta with Pine Nuts and Smoked Trout or Spinach, Lavender, and Goat Cheese Strata (see pages 95 and 115). This side also goes well with grilled meats and fish.

Carrots and Snap Peas with Ginger Butter

SERVES 12

A STEP UP FROM YOUR MOTHER'S PEAS AND CARROTS! QUICK AND EASY TO MAKE, THE BLENDED GINGER BUTTER ADDS A NICE TOUCH TO THIS COLORFUL, CRUNCHY SIDE DISH. GRATED GINGERROOT BLENDS NICELY WITH THE BUTTER—YOU'LL NEED TO BUY A LARGER ROOT THAN YOU WOULD IF YOU WERE MINCING IT.

¼ CUP BUTTER
¼ CUP GRATED FRESH GINGER
2 POUNDS CARROTS, PEELED AND SLICED INTO ¼-INCH-THICK DIAGONALS
2 TABLESPOONS SALT
2 POUNDS SUGAR SNAP PEAS, TRIMMED
2 TABLESPOONS FRESH LEMON JUICE
   SALT AND PEPPER TO TASTE

GARNISH SUGGESTIONS
  (CHOOSE ONE)

    CILANTRO, CHOPPED
    FRESH CHIVES, CHOPPED
    ITALIAN PARSLEY, CHOPPED

Melt butter in a large sauté pan over medium-low heat. Stir in grated ginger. Add carrots to melted butter and ginger. Increase heat to medium, cover pan, and cook carrots until barely tender, 5 to 10 minutes.

While carrots are cooking, fill a soup pot with water and bring to a boil. Add salt and the snap peas. Cook for 2 minutes. Strain and rinse with cold water to stop cooking. Set aside until needed. Combine snap peas with carrots and toss to coat thoroughly with ginger butter. Season with lemon juice, salt, and pepper.

As a cook, it's easy to spend all your time on the main dish and neglect the side dishes. This recipe elevates the side dish to something special. I served it with flank steak marinated in red wine and a glass of merlot on the side.

–Janet on Parkside Drive

Fresh Green Beans with Orange Vinaigrette

SERVES 12

BRIGHT AND CRISP AS A SUNNY SPRING DAY. WE LOVE THIS COMBINATION OF FLAVORS. TRY THE SAME VINAIGRETTE ON STEAMED BROCCOLI AND CARROTS, TOO.

ORANGE VINAIGRETTE

2   SHALLOTS, MINCED
2   TABLESPOONS WHITE WINE
    VINEGAR
2   ORANGES, ZESTED AND JUICED
¼   CUP OLIVE OIL
1   TEASPOON MAPLE SYRUP
    SALT AND PEPPER TO TASTE

BEANS

3   POUNDS FRESH GREEN BEANS
    (FROZEN OPTIONAL), TRIMMED
2   TABLESPOONS SALT

GARNISH SUGGESTIONS

ORANGES, SLICED
FRESH CHIVES, CHOPPED
FRESH CHIVE FLOWERS

ORANGE VINAIGRETTE In a medium bowl, marinate the shallots in the vinegar for 10 minutes. Then whisk in remaining ingredients to complete the vinaigrette and set aside until needed.

BEANS If beans are longer than 3 inches, cut in half. Bring a soup pot of cold water to a boil. Add salt. Drop half of green beans into rapidly boiling water. Cook until beans are bright green and barely tender. Remove pot from heat and, using a sieve or strainer with a handle, scoop out beans. Return water to rapid boil and repeat for the rest of the beans. Divide beans among serving dishes and toss with vinaigrette.

> Tangy orange sauce—mmm. This dish looks beautiful, and it's an easy way to spruce up a simple vegetable.
>
> –Jennifer on 23rd Street

Roasted Tomatoes Stuffed with Goat Cheese and Sage

SERVES 12

AN EXPLOSION OF TANGY GOAT CHEESE SEASONED WITH FRIED SAGE AND GARLIC MAKES EVEN WINTER TOMATOES SPECIAL. THE BREAD CRUMB CRUST OFFERS A CRISPY COUNTERPART TO THE SMOOTH, RICH FILLING. TRY EXPERIMENTING WITH THESE TOMATOES ON THE GRILL—LEAVE THEM ON UNTIL THEY'RE GOOEY AND READY TO FALL APART!

6	CLOVES GARLIC, SEPARATED BUT NOT PEELED
¼	CUP BUTTER
36	FRESH SAGE LEAVES
8	OUNCES GOAT CHEESE
¼	CUP SOUR CREAM
	SALT AND PEPPER TO TASTE
6	MEDIUM TOMATOES,* HALVED HORIZONTALLY AND SEEDED
¾	CUP BREAD CRUMBS, HOMEMADE (VERY LIGHTLY TOASTED)**
¼	CUP GRATED PARMESAN

Cook garlic in nonstick pan on medium heat for 10 minutes to "dry roast" until soft; turn occasionally. Cool. Peel and mince.

Melt butter in medium sauté pan over medium-low heat and sauté sage in two batches until crisp but still green, 10 to 15 minutes. Stir occasionally so the sage and butter don't burn.

Preheat oven to 425 degrees F.

Whip together goat cheese, sour cream, salt, and pepper in a small bowl. Stir in the garlic and ¾ of the sage leaves (crumbled). Reserve the rest of the sage leaves (whole) as garnish.

Lightly salt tomato halves and drain, cut side down, on a dishcloth to remove excess moisture. Spread a tablespoon of cheese mixture on each tomato half, pressing it into the tomato cavities.

Combine bread crumbs and Parmesan in a small bowl and top each tomato half with 1 tablespoon of crumb mixture. Spray nonstick spray on a sheet pan and place tomatoes on it. Roast for 15 minutes, or until tops are golden brown. Garnish with reserved sage leaves.

> Lovely red cups of texture and flavor. These stuffed tomatoes taste even better than they look.
>
> –Vida on Berkeley Street

*If you're using small homegrown tomatoes, serve twice as many and roast or grill them whole. Just remove the core and hollow out the insides a little to make room for the cheese stuffing.

**See Making Bread Crumbs on page 91.

Cauliflower Clouds with Julienne Brussels Sprouts

SERVES 12

HERE YOU WILL BARELY RECOGNIZE CAULIFLOWER AND BRUSSELS SPROUTS AS THEMSELVES—THEY ARE PREPARED IN A TOTALLY NONTRADITIONAL FASHION. CAULIFLOWER IS COOKED AND PUREED WITH POTATOES UNTIL CREAMY, AND THE BRUSSELS SPROUTS ARE TRANSFORMED BY THE WAY YOU'LL CUT THEM. THE END RESULT IS A CLOUDLIKE PRESENTATION WITH A PRETTY GREEN "NEST" OF JULIENNE BRUSSELS SPROUTS POPPING OUT OF THE CENTER.

CAULIFLOWER CLOUDS

2   CUPS CHICKEN OR VEGETABLE BROTH

6   CLOVES GARLIC, MINCED

12   OUNCES POTATOES, PEELED AND DICED

3   HEADS CAULIFLOWER, SEPARATED INTO MEDIUM-SIZE FLORETS WITH LARGE STEMS CUT OFF

12   OUNCES CREAM CHEESE

JULIENNE BRUSSELS SPROUTS

4   TABLESPOONS BUTTER

4   TABLESPOONS OLIVE OIL

¾   OUNCE FRESH SAGE LEAVES, CHOPPED

1½   POUNDS BRUSSELS SPROUTS, JULIENNED*

     SALT AND PEPPER TO TASTE

CAULIFLOWER CLOUDS In a soup pot, bring broth to a boil. Add garlic and potatoes, and give a little stir. Then place cauliflower in the pot, lower heat, cover, and simmer for 20 to 30 minutes, until everything is completely tender. While cooking, stir occasionally from the bottom, as if you were folding egg whites, to ensure even cooking. This takes a while because you have so much in one pot. You may also divide the vegetables into two pots, which will take less cooking time.

Puree cauliflower mixture with cream cheese in batches with a handheld (immersion) blender or in batches in a blender until smooth and creamy. If you need more liquid to make it blend, add more broth a little at a time. Portion pureed cauliflower into co-op dishes and leave in a 200 degrees F oven until needed. (If you are short on oven space and want to make this before you need it, reheat on stove in soup pot over medium-low heat, stirring often.)

JULIENNE BRUSSELS SPROUTS Melt butter and heat olive oil in large pot over medium heat. Add remaining ingredients. Stir often and cook until Brussels sprouts are heated through and tender, about 5 minutes. Make a well in the center of the pureed cauliflower and place the Brussels sprouts in the well, leaving a margin of cauliflower all around so you have a beautiful presentation.

*To julienne Brussels sprouts, cut each in half through the ends. Place half cut side down and slice thinly.

> Surprise! This dish is absolutely fantastic. Pureed cauliflower would not be on my list of top foods, but I loved this. The combination of smooth, creamy mashed potato-like cauliflower with the slight bite of the Brussels sprouts was perfect. My kids gobbled it up, and so did I!
>
> –Janet on Parkside Drive

Swiss Chard and Potato Gratin with Goat Cheese

SERVES 12

DELICIOUS AND SATISFYING, THIS DISH STARTS WITH A BASIC POTATO GRATIN AND LAYERS OUR FAVORITE INGREDIENTS FROM ONE OF OUR FAVORITE CHEFS, DEBORAH MADISON. GOAT CHEESE BRINGS A CERTAIN SOPHISTICATION TO A SIMPLE GRATIN THAT YOU PREPARE AND BAKE RIGHT INSIDE THE CO-OP DISHES.

3 POUNDS YUKON GOLD POTATOES (OR OTHER THIN-SKINNED WAXY POTATO)
1/3 CUP BUTTER
3 ONIONS, SLICED
6 CLOVES GARLIC, MINCED
3 POUNDS SWISS CHARD, STEMS AND LEAVES CHOPPED* SEPARATELY
12 OUNCES GOAT CHEESE, CRUMBLED
2 TABLESPOONS SALT

GRATIN TOPPING

3 TABLESPOONS BUTTER
3 CLOVES GARLIC, MINCED
3 CUPS WHOLE-WHEAT BREAD CRUMBS, HOMEMADE** (NOT TOASTED)
3 TABLESPOONS BUTTER
3 TABLESPOONS FLOUR
3 CUPS HOT MILK
SALT AND PEPPER TO TASTE

GARNISH SUGGESTIONS:

ITALIAN PARSLEY SPRIGS
FRESH CHIVES, CHOPPED

Parboil whole potatoes in skins until barely tender, cool, and slice into 1/4-inch slices.

Heat butter in a large soup pot over medium heat. Sauté onions, garlic, and only half of chard **stems** until nearly soft. Stir in chard **leaves,** cover, and lower heat to let leaves wilt down. Stir occasionally until leaves are uniformly wilted and bright green. Remove from heat. Stir cheese into chard mixture and season to taste with salt.

GRATIN TOPPING Heat butter in a large sauté pan over medium heat. Sauté garlic and bread crumbs 1 minute while stirring constantly. Remove them to a bowl.

Preheat oven to 400 degrees F.

Wipe out the large skillet and melt butter over low heat. Stir in the flour and cook for a minute or so, stirring so it won't brown. Whisk in hot milk and cook over medium heat 6 to 10 minutes until thickened. Salt and pepper to taste. Stir sauce into chard mixture.

ASSEMBLE GRATIN Layer half of chard mixture into rectangle co-op serving dishes. Layer all of the potatoes on top of chard. Place remaining chard on potatoes and top with bread crumbs. Bake for 25 to 30 minutes. The gratin should be bubbling and golden on top.

*See Showing Chard Who's Boss on page 85.

**See Making Bread Crumbs on page 91.

Serve this wonderful dish with a soup or alongside grilled fish or meat.

Roasted Sweet Potatoes with Orange Chipotle Glaze

SERVES 12

MAPLE SYRUP AND CHIPOTLE CHILES ARE BOTH NATURALS WITH SWEET POTATOES. SO WHY CHOOSE BETWEEN THEM? WE COMBINE THESE FLAVORS IN A LOVELY GLAZE THAT CARAMELIZES IN THE OVEN. IF YOU WOULD RATHER GO STRICTLY SWEET, LEAVE OUT THE CHIPOTLE PEPPERS.

9	OUNCES ORANGE JUICE CONCENTRATE, THAWED
1/3	CUP OLIVE OIL
3	TABLESPOONS MAPLE SYRUP
2	TABLESPOONS CINNAMON
1/2	TEASPOON FRESHLY GRATED NUTMEG
1 1/2	TABLESPOONS CHIPOTLE PEPPERS IN ADOBO SAUCE (OPTIONAL), PUREED
50	OUNCES SMALL GARNET YAMS*

GARNISH SUGGESTION

    LIMES, SLICED

Preheat oven to 425 degrees F.

Combine all ingredients except yams and mix.

Cut yams from tip to tip into 3/4-inch wedges, leaving the skin on. Place wedges on 2 foiled sheet pans. Paint the glaze on the yams using a pastry brush. Bake for 60 minutes, or until fork tender. Divide yams into the round co-op dishes.

*To save time, you can partially cook the yams in the microwave. Do this before you cut them. Ten minutes on high for this amount works pretty well. Let cool after you take them out of the microwave and cut as described above. Then brush with glaze and cook in the oven for 25 to 30 minutes, or until tender.

Our kids actually liked the spicy chipotles in this dish!

–Sarah on 16th Street

Mixed Greens Sauté with Cannellini Beans and White Balsamic Vinaigrette

SERVES 12

LEAFY GREENS CAN VARY IN TASTE, FROM SPICY/TANGY MUSTARD GREENS TO MILD SPINACH. BY BLENDING A VARIETY OF GREENS, YOU CAN ADJUST THE FLAVORS TO SUIT YOUR PREFERENCE. WHITE BALSAMIC VINEGAR AND RED PEPPER FLAKES ADD BALANCE AND A LITTLE KICK.

3   CUPS WATER

2   BUNCHES MUSTARD OR TURNIP GREENS, ROUGHLY CHOPPED

2   BUNCHES SWISS CHARD OR BEET GREENS, LEAVES AND STEMS CHOPPED*

16   OUNCES FRESH SPINACH, LARGE STEMS REMOVED

2   TABLESPOONS OLIVE OIL

6   CLOVES GARLIC, MINCED

½   TEASPOON RED PEPPER FLAKES
     SALT AND PEPPER TO TASTE

30   OUNCES CANNED CANNELLINI BEANS (OR LARGE NAVY BEANS), DRAINED AND RINSED

1   TABLESPOON FRESH LEMON JUICE

2   TABLESPOONS WHITE BALSAMIC VINEGAR

GARNISH SUGGESTION

LEMONS, SLICED

Heat water in a large soup pot until boiling. Add mustard or turnip greens and simmer for 7 minutes, or until barely tender.

Cut the chard stems in half lengthwise and slice them thinly. Add chopped leaves and stems to the mustard/turnip greens in the pot. Simmer another 5 minutes.

Add spinach leaves and cook briefly until wilted. Drain any excess water from the greens and set aside.

Heat oil over medium heat in a small sauté pan. Sauté garlic about 30 seconds. Add pepper flakes and remove pan from heat after another 30 seconds. Pour oil mixture over cooked greens and toss to coat. Add salt and pepper to taste.

Gently warm beans in a saucepan over medium heat or in the microwave. Toss beans with lemon juice and vinegar. Divide greens among serving dishes. Top each dish with beans.

*See Showing Chard Who's Boss page 85.

> Growing up in the South, we always ate our greens. It's fun to find new and flavorful ways to serve them.
>
> –Carl on 25th Street

As an option, a firm fish such as grilled snapper or salmon is great on top of this bed of sautéed mixed greens.

Roasted Beets, Carrots, and Shallots

SERVES 12

THE VIBRANT COLORS OF BEETS AND CARROTS TOGETHER DECORATE ANY MEAL. THEIR DELICIOUS FLAVORS COMPLEMENT AND ENHANCE EACH OTHER IN THIS VERY HEALTHY AND SATISFYING DISH.

ROASTED BEETS

- 12 FRESH BEETS (SAVE GREENS FOR GARNISH IF DESIRED)
- 2 TABLESPOONS BALSAMIC VINEGAR*
- 2 TABLESPOONS OLIVE OIL
  SALT AND PEPPER TO TASTE

CARROTS AND SHALLOTS

- 4 POUNDS CARROTS, PEELED AND SLICED DIAGONALLY
- 3 TABLESPOONS BUTTER, MELTED
- 2 TABLESPOONS BROWN SUGAR
- 1 POUND SHALLOTS, PEELED AND HALVED OR QUARTERED
- 2 TABLESPOONS OLIVE OIL
  SALT AND PEPPER TO TASTE

GARNISH SUGGESTIONS
(CHOOSE ONE)

GREEN ONIONS, SLICED
FRESH CHIVES, CHOPPED

BEET GREEN GARNISH (OPTIONAL)

- 1½ TABLESPOONS BUTTER
- 1½ TABLESPOONS OLIVE OIL
  BEET GREENS, CHOPPED

ROASTED BEETS Boil whole beets with skins on until barely tender, about 45 minutes. Remove from pan and peel when cool enough to handle. Use gloves to avoid staining your fingers.

Preheat oven to 375 degrees F.

Cut each beet into about 8 wedges. Toss beets in a bowl with the vinegar, olive oil, salt, and pepper, and pour them onto a sheet pan. Roast beets at 375 degrees F for 15 to 20 minutes, until slightly caramelized.

CARROTS AND SHALLOTS While the beets are cooking, prep the carrots and combine them with butter and brown sugar in a bowl. Stir to evenly coat carrots.

Prepare shallots so they are about the same size as the carrot slices. Toss with olive oil.

Mix carrots, shallots, salt, and pepper together and pour onto 1 or 2 sheet pans. Roast at 375 degrees F for 20 to 25 minutes, until carrots are crisp-tender.

> Warm and earthy, like your favorite sweater on a fall day.
>
> —Sarah on 16th Street

Divide carrots and shallots among serving dishes. Top with beets.

BEET GREEN GARNISH Heat butter and oil in a sauté pan on medium. Add greens and sauté until greens are wilted and stems tender, 5 to 10 minutes. Arrange greens around the edges of each serving dish.

*See Special Ingredients for the Co-op Cook on page 155.

Whole Wheat Couscous with Orange Zest, Dried Cranberries, and Pumpkin Seeds

SERVES 12

THIS ORANGE-INFUSED COUSCOUS WITH TANGY DRIED CRANBERRIES AND SWEET RAISINS MAKES THE PERFECT FOIL FOR CHICKEN OR PORK. IT CAN BE SERVED HOT, CHILLED, OR AT ROOM TEMPERATURE. WE REALLY LIKE THE FLAVOR OF WHOLE-WHEAT COUSCOUS, BUT YOU CAN SUBSTITUTE ANY COUSCOUS YOU PREFER.

3	CUPS CHICKEN OR VEGETABLE BROTH
3	ORANGES, ZESTED AND JUICED (RESERVE ZEST)
4	CUPS WHOLE WHEAT (SEMOLINA) COUSCOUS
1½	CUPS GOLDEN RAISINS
1½	CUPS DRIED CRANBERRIES
1	TEASPOON SALT
1½	CUPS PUMPKIN SEEDS, TOASTED

GARNISH SUGGESTIONS

FRESH CHIVES, CHOPPED
  (USE KITCHEN SCISSORS)
FRESH MINT LEAVES, CHOPPED

Bring broth and orange juice to a boil. Remove from heat, stirring in couscous and fruit. Cover and remove from heat for 10 minutes. Fluff couscous with a fork.

Add salt and pumpkin seeds along with the reserved orange zest, and fluff again to thoroughly distribute these ingredients. Divide couscous among serving dishes.

> We love the different textures in this dish—especially the roasted pumpkin seeds.
>
> –Lee on Riverview Drive

Quinoa with Fresh Corn, Tomatoes, and Scallions

SERVES 12

QUINOA IS AN ANCIENT GRAIN, HIGH IN PROTEIN, YET DELICATE IN FLAVOR AND TEXTURE.
THIS PAIRING MAKES A GREAT SUMMER GRAIN DISH THAT CAN BE SERVED WARM OR AT ROOM TEMPERATURE.

8	EARS FRESH CORN, SHUCKED*
4	CUPS CHICKEN OR VEGETABLE BROTH
1	CUP WATER
6	RESERVED CORNCOBS
3	CUPS QUINOA
1	PINT CHERRY TOMATOES, HALVED OR QUARTERED (IF LARGE)
1½	CUPS GREEN ONIONS, SLICED
3	TABLESPOONS OLIVE OIL
1½	LEMONS, ZESTED AND JUICED
1½	TEASPOONS SALT
¾	TEASPOON PEPPER

GARNISH SUGGESTIONS
(CHOOSE ONE)

ITALIAN PARSLEY, CHOPPED
CILANTRO, CHOPPED

Using a sharp knife, slice the corn kernels off each cob. Place corn in a large bowl. Reserve corncobs for broth.

Heat broth and water over medium heat in a soup pot. If using fresh corn, add corncobs and simmer for 10 to 15 minutes. Remove corncobs from broth and discard. (The dish still tastes great when you omit the cornob step.)

Rinse quinoa in cold water 3 times, using a sieve between each rinsing. Bring broth back to a boil and add the quinoa. Simmer, uncovered, for 10 minutes, until grains are almost tender but a little bit of crunch remains. Drain any excess liquid and add quinoa to the large bowl with corn kernels.

Gently stir tomatoes and onions into quinoa.

Combine remaining ingredients in a small bowl and then pour over quinoa, fluffing to thoroughly distribute these ingredients. Divide quinoa among serving dishes.

*Corn: Cut fresh kernels off the cob or substitute 1 cup frozen and thawed corn for each ear.

Lucky my wife was out of town—I got to eat it all myself.

–Carl on 25th Street

Wild Rice and Chickpea Salad

Serves 12

Here is a wild treatment of wild rice—colorful snap peas, yellow pear tomatoes, and chickpeas make this an endlessly useful cold salad when you want to raise eyebrows on a Wednesday night. Challenge your tasters to divine the ingredients in this dressing—we doubt they'll succeed, and your chef's mystique will remain.

Rice

2½ cups wild rice
7½ cups water

Wild All-Star Dressing

½ cup olive oil
½ cup walnut or hazelnut oil
⅓ cup apple cider vinegar
¼ cup sour cream
½ cup dill pickle relish
2 teaspoons maple syrup
   Salt and pepper to taste

Vegetables

¼ cup salt
4 cups sugar snap peas, trimmed
22 ounces canned chickpeas (garbanzo beans), rinsed and drained
1 cup finely chopped red onion*
1 pint yellow pear or cherry tomatoes, sliced in half
3 tablespoons Italian parsley, chopped

Garnish Suggestions

Hazelnuts, toasted** and chopped
Italian parsley sprigs

Rice Simmer for 50 to 60 minutes in soup pot until rice is tender; drain and cool. Place in a large bowl.

Wild All-Star Dressing Whisk ingredients together in a medium bowl.

Vegetables Fill a large pot with water and bring to a boil. Add salt and the snap peas. Cook for 2 minutes. Strain and rinse with cold water to stop cooking. Add to large bowl with rice.

Combine chickpeas, onion, tomatoes, and parsley with rice and snap peas, and toss with salad dressing. Place in co-op dishes. Chill for 1 hour or serve at room temperature.

*If you're feeding kids who don't care for raw onion, slice the red onion in rings and place on top of salad so they may be eaten or not.

**Toasting Hazelnuts: To make it easy to remove the papery skin and intensify their flavor, toast hazelnuts in an oven at 375 degrees F for about 10 minutes, watching carefully. Rub them in a dishtowel after toasting, and most of the skins will flake right off.

> I admit I was skeptical about the ingredients in this dressing. But I was blown away by how good it was when it all came together.
>
> –Vida on Berkeley Street

Bulgur with Artichoke Hearts, Lemon, and Goat Cheese

SERVES 12

TANGY, CREAMY, AND NUTTY FLAVORS COMBINE IN THIS QUICK SIDE DISH. A VERSATILE ACCOMPANIMENT FOR A MAIN DISH SALAD OR A GRILLED MEAT. SERVE HOT OR AT ROOM TEMPERATURE.

3 TABLESPOONS OLIVE OIL

3 MEDIUM LEEKS*, WHITE AND LIGHT GREEN PARTS, THINLY SLICED

2⅓ CUPS BULGUR WHEAT, MEDIUM COARSENESS

3½ CUPS CHICKEN OR VEGETABLE BROTH

28 OUNCES CANNED ARTICHOKE HEART QUARTERS, DRAINED

2 LEMONS, ZESTED AND JUICED

⅔ CUP FRESH CHIVES, CHOPPED
Salt and pepper to taste

6 OUNCES GOAT CHEESE, CRUMBLED

GARNISH SUGGESTIONS

HAZELNUTS OR PINE NUTS, TOASTED
LEMON SLICES
FRESH CHIVE FLOWERS
FRESH MINT SPRIGS

Heat oil in a soup pot over medium heat. Add leeks and stir until softened, 5 minutes.

Add bulgur to leeks and stir until bulgur is well coated with oil. Add broth and bring to a boil. Turn the heat to low, cover, and simmer about 15 to 20 minutes, until bulgur grains are cooked but still a bit chewy. Remove from heat and drain off any cooking liquid that remains.

Gently combine artichoke hearts, lemon zest and juice, chives, salt, and pepper with cooked bulgur.

Fold the goat cheese in last. Divide among serving dishes.

*See Washing Leeks on page 76 in Roasted Asparagus Soup.

> We added toasted pine nuts for some extra crunch. I will definitely make this again!
>
> –Lee on Riverview Drive

Wheat Berries with Roasted Red Peppers and Carrots

SERVES 12

WHEAT BERRIES ARE A POWERHOUSE GRAIN PACKED WITH FIBER, ZINC, AND B6 VITAMINS—THEY'RE VERY HEALTHY AND VERSATILE. IN OUR SALAD, HAZELNUTS AND HAZELNUT OIL ADD A GREAT NUTTY FLAVOR TO THE WHEAT BERRIES' TEXTURE. THE UNIQUE DRESSING GETS PUNCH FROM A DASH OF ROASTED RED PEPPER AND A LITTLE FETA CHEESE, WHICH ARE REPEATED IN THE DISH, ADDING ANOTHER LAYER OF FLAVORS.

3½ CUPS HARD WHEAT BERRIES*, RINSED

7 CUPS WATER

3 CUPS CHICKEN BROTH

ROASTED RED PEPPER AND FETA DRESSING

½ CUP APPLE CIDER VINEGAR

⅓ CUP OLIVE OIL

3 TABLESPOONS HAZELNUT OR WALNUT OIL (MORE OLIVE OIL IS OKAY)

⅓ OF A ROASTED RED PEPPER, FROM A JAR OR HOMEMADE, CHOPPED

1 SHALLOT, CHOPPED

2½ OUNCES FETA CHEESE

PUTTING THE SALAD TOGETHER

3⅔ ROASTED RED PEPPERS, FROM A JAR OR HOMEMADE, DICED

3 CARROTS, DICED

1 CUP RED CABBAGE, DICED

3 TABLESPOONS CILANTRO, CHOPPED

1 HEAD ROMAINE

GARNISH SUGGESTIONS

HAZELNUTS, TOASTED** AND CHOPPED

FETA CHEESE, CRUMBLED

CILANTRO SPRIGS

Combine wheat berries, water, and chicken broth in a large soup pot and bring to a boil. Reduce heat and simmer, covered, for 50 to 55 minutes until done. Take off heat and allow to cool. Place in a large bowl.

ROASTED RED PEPPER AND FETA DRESSING Combine ingredients together in blender.

PUTTING THE SALAD TOGETHER Add red peppers, carrots, cabbage, and cilantro with dressing to wheat berries and mix.

Line co-op side dishes with lettuce leaves and top with salad. Serve cold or at room temperature.

*Hard wheat berries can often be found in supermarkets with a good bulk section.

**See Toasting Hazelnuts on page 147.

Mango Basmati Rice with Mint and Ginger

SERVES 12

WE THINK OF MANGOES AS WINTER PEACHES—A GREAT WAY TO ADD SOMETHING EXOTIC TO A WEEKDAY MEAL—AND WONDERFUL WITH GRILLED SALMON OR CHICKEN.

¼   CUP BUTTER

¼   CUP GRATED FRESH GINGER

1   OUNCE FRESH MINT LEAVES, MINCED (DIVIDED)

2¼   CUPS WHITE BASMATI RICE*

1   TEASPOON SALT

3¾   CUPS WATER

2   MANGOES, FRESH OR FROM A JAR, DICED

SALT TO TASTE

GARNISH SUGGESTIONS

FRESH MINT SPRIGS

LIME SLICES

Heat butter over medium heat in a large saucepan. Stir in the ginger and half the mint leaves. Warm them for 30 seconds. Add rice and stir to coat.

Add salt and water. Bring to a boil. Cover and simmer for 15 minutes, or until rice is tender. Remove from heat and let stand, covered, for 10 minutes.

Add mangoes and the rest of the mint. Adjust seasonings. Divide among serving dishes.

*You may also use brown basmati rice for a nuttier flavor. Increase the simmer time to 40 minutes or follow the package directions.

Serve with our Salmon with Fresh Strawberry Relish (see page 99).

QUICK SIDES AND EXTRAS

LITTLE THINGS MAKE DINNER TWICE AS NICE

Sometimes we make a good dinner and wish we had just one more thing to round off our menu. Here are a few of our favorite standbys—these little extras are never expected but always appreciated.

SWEETS

Memorable cookies: Add a twist to your favorite chocolate chip cookie recipe with orange zest, dried cherries, coconut, or spices (cinnamon, nutmeg, cardamom).

High-alert brownies: Prepare brownies from a mix and add espresso in place of the water.

Homemade ice cream sandwiches: Take brownies or cookies and your favorite ice cream, add chocolate, caramel, or a fruit sauce between layers. Assemble and freeze hard ahead of time.

Hand-dipped fruits and cookies: Dip strawberries, dried apricots, shortbread cookies, Oreos, or gingersnaps in melted chocolate for a fun and delicious presentation. To melt chocolate, place chocolate chips or sweetened baking chocolate in a double boiler or use the microwave at half power. Check after every minute and stir until just melted. Line a sheet pan with wax paper or a nonstick baking mat. Dip selected treats in melted chocolate and then place on the wax paper. Chill for at least 30 minutes.

APPETIZERS

Bean Dips as a Starter: These are very easy—just put everything together in a food processor. Jazz up traditional bean dips like hummus by adding roasted red peppers, pesto, artichoke hearts, or olives, and puree with different kinds of beans. Add a splash of lemon or lime juice, maybe some honey or agave nectar, and salt and pepper. Serve with pita bread, dried pita chips, bagel chips, crackers, vegetable crudités, and antipasto platters.

Vegetable Crudités and Antipasto Platters: Not in the mood to make a salad? Arrange a colorful variety of **fresh vegetables** or antipasto fare in your co-op dishes. Serve with a thick, creamy dressing, aioli, or a bean dip in a hollowed half cabbage, tomato, or bell pepper for an easy but impressive touch.

Include baby turnips, small romaine leaves, endive, beets, artichoke hearts, cherry tomatoes, julienne bell peppers, fresh carrots, cauliflower, broccoli, asparagus, snap peas, snow peas, green beans, or zucchini.

A great **antipasto platter** can include prosciutto, salamis, sliced meats, cheeses, marinated vegetables, pickled vegetables, olives, small red boiled potatoes with salt, sliced or quartered hard-cooked eggs, chick peas, shrimp, or smoked fish.

ACCOMPANIMENTS FOR BREAD

Make a little something extra to serve with bread. If you're not baking the bread yourself, choose a good-quality artisan bread.

Herb-Garlic Bread: Combine $1/2$ cup of softened butter and $1/4$ cup of olive oil with a teaspoon each of minced garlic, dried oregano, rosemary, dill seed, thyme, and basil. Spread on split baguettes and grill or broil until browned.

Manchego Cheese with Almond-Fig Loaf and Quince Jam—homemade or from your farmers market.

Goat Cheese Crostini from our Asian Chard Soup recipe (see page 84).

Bruschetta toppings—traditional tomato and garlic or olive tapenade from our Roast Beef Sandwiches (see page 125).

FRESH FRUIT

Fresh-cut fruit is always a welcome side dish. Mix it up with these ideas:

Mangoes in a splash of lime juice, clementines unpeeled and wrapped up nicely, frozen grapes on a hot summer day, or fresh ripe pineapple mixed with other fruits.

Forbidden Fruit: Toss watermelon and basil with a little tequila or toss dark rum with a dash of sugar and cinnamon with fruits such as grapes, pineapple, citrus sections, and apples.

> From the Neighborhood
>
> I know my son is spending too much time with Andy when he fills the ice cube trays and puts strawberries in the centers of each cube.
>
> —Sheila on State Street

ETHNIC EXTRAS

Add special items that go with your ethnic meal. We've seen kids respond to these little extras, making them more excited about trying new foods.

Mexican—Packaged Chiclets (in Mexican food aisle), a Mexican candle, Mexican wedding cookies, or homemade guacamole for a side (see our Guacamole recipe from Tacos à la Carte (on page 87).

Chinese—Fortune cookies (Asian aisle, look for them in a box).

Thai—Make Mango Lassies (mangoes, yogurt, and sugar over crushed ice).

Indian—Include prepared chutneys or try making your own. Or make homemade yogurt.

Here are a few pantry items every weeknight cook should know about! Elevate your cooking with no extra effort—try some of our favorite seasonings and gourmet time-savers.

Agave nectar, made from the juice of the agave plant, has a naturally sweet flavor. It dissolves quickly, doesn't crystallize, and has a low glycemic index.

Ancho chile powder is from dried poblano chiles and has a smoky, sweet chile flavor with mild heat—or substitute with mild chile powder.

Curry paste—Andy loves a brand called Patak's, which comes in mild to hot and a variety of spice flavors. Look for it in the aisle with Indian foods.

Ginger in jars from Christopher Ranch is a great shortcut for fresh ginger because it is not stringy or chunky.

Fig balsamic vinegar by Made In Napa Valley is a luscious, smooth balsamic that adds depth and richness to marinades, dressings, and sauces.

Fire-roasted tomatoes by Muir Glen are a staple in our cupboards. They are available whole, diced, or sauced, and add a smoky depth of flavor to soups, stews, and hearty tomato-based sauces.

Lemon Grass Puree is available in small tubes in the produce section of many grocers, near the fresh herbs. It keeps well in your refrigerator and is much easier to use than lemon grass stalks.

Fresh lime juice—skip all the squeezing with Santa Cruz Lime Juice. It is 100 percent juice with no sugar added and is not from concentrate.

Smoked Spanish paprika, *pimentón ahumado,* has an incredible magical flavor that will completely transform your dish; you will see that it is very different from your everyday paprika.

Pasilla chile powder is from dark, fruity pasilla chile peppers with medium heat. If you need to substitute, look for New Mexico chile powders.

Essential Tools

Highly recommended tools for co-op cooks

Great kitchen tools are something you build up gradually, like a killer CD collection. Start with the essentials and then add as you can. Owning a huge bowl, pot, and pan from the very start will help avoid the frustration of too much volume in a small vessel.

Essentials
- ◯ A giant stainless steel bowl (5 quarts)
- ◯ A large soup pot with lid
- ◯ An instant-read meat thermometer

Recommended
- ◯ Very large sauté pan or oven-proof skillet (1 or 2)
- ◯ Food processor (Cuisinart), blender, or hand-held blender (immersion blender)
- ◯ Microplane grater
- ◯ Sheet pans with rolled rims, 18 x 13 inches (2 or 3)
- ◯ A large heavy-duty roasting pan
- ◯ Heat-resistant silicone spatulas and serving spoons
- ◯ Kitchen shears
- ◯ A big ladle, 1 cup size
- ◯ Double burner pancake griddle

Metric Conversion Chart

Liquid and Dry Measures

U.S.	Canadian	Australian
¼ teaspoon	1 mL	1 ml
½ teaspoon	2 mL	2 ml
1 teaspoon	5 mL	5 ml
1 tablespoon	15 mL	20 ml
¼ cup	50 mL	60 ml
⅓ cup	75 mL	80 ml
½ cup	125 mL	125 ml
⅔ cup	150 mL	170 ml
¾ cup	175 mL	190 ml
1 cup	250 mL	250 ml
1 quart	1 liter	1 litre

Temperature Conversion Chart

Fahrenheit	Celsius
250	120
275	140
300	150
325	160
350	180
375	190
400	200
425	220
450	230
475	240
500	260

RECOMMENDED READING

READ THE SAME BOOKS TO GET IN THE SPIRIT

As our dinner co-ops started picking up steam, we found ourselves reading food books in our book club, at the beach, and on the plane. Here are some of the most inspired and entertaining food books we've seen.

Garlic and Sapphires: The Secret Life of a Critic in Disguise
Ruth Reichl

Reichl takes us with her into restaurants across New York City to show that the experience of a good meal only begins with how it tastes. She goes to the mat for the common man or woman, brilliantly and publicly holding the restaurant business accountable for how they really make people feel every day.

Animal, Vegetable, Miracle: A Year of Food Life
Barbara Kingsolver with Steven L. Hopp and Camille Kingsolver

A rock star among book clubs, novelist Barbara Kingsolver tells the tale of her family's move to southern Appalachia in a quest to realign their lives with the food chain. They spend an unforgettable year raising and growing, canning, and preserving while deepening their connection to the natural world.

Soul of a Chef: The Journey Toward Perfection
Michael Ruhlman

Ruhlman introduces us to our main man Chef Thomas Keller and allows us to spend some time at The French Laundry. He takes us in real-time to the Culinary Institute of America, where he follows a few beloved regional chefs of unquestionable skill as they proceed to fail the incredibly rigorous Master Chef Exam. Should perfection be pursued at the expense of warmth and hospitality? For us weeknight cooks, the answer is no.

Heat
Bill Buford

One of the themes in this book is "cooking with love." When you cook with love, every dish is a unique event—you never allow yourself to forget that a person is waiting to eat your food, made with your hands.

Julie and Julia: My Year of Cooking Dangerously
Julie Powell

A funny and triumphant tell-all of a woman at a crossroads who uses a classic Julia Child cookbook to lead her out of the darkness.

Forms and Worksheets

Getting Started Checklist

○ Identify good cooks who live nearby.

○ Complete and talk through Compatibility Surveys.

○ Review Food Preferences and finalize list of "no thanks" ingredients.

○ Finalize your circle of chefs.

○ Host a kick-off meeting.

○ Decide on a delivery schedule.

○ Agree on portion sizes.

○ Review Food Safety.

○ Complete and exchange Member Profiles.

○ Buy containers.

○ Launch it and start cooking! Get together every now and then to give feedback.

First Meeting Prep Worksheet

Complete as much as you can before your first meeting and then talk through it face-to-face. Also complete your Co-op Member Profile now and turn it in to the organizing chef.

NAME_____

My ideal night to cook is
M   T   W   TH   (F)

My second choice would be
M   T   W   TH   (F)

It's undesirable or not possible for me to cook on
M   T   W   TH   (F)

After talking it over with the group, I will cook on
M   T   W   TH   (F)

The earliest I think I could deliver meals to the group would be at _____ p.m.

If you drop off any later than _____ p.m., we've probably already eaten something.

If you need to deliver early, someone is usually home by _____.

We have all agreed to deliver between
5:00 and 5:30   6:00 and 6:30
5:30 and 6:00   7:00 and 7:30

We will make and deliver _____ portions per household.

We will always deliver dressing with salad ___ No ___ Yes.

I need to remember to bring up the following questions or issues at the first meeting:

I need to buy (number) _____ of containers by (date) _____. Or (name) _____ will buy them for the group, and we all will reimburse her.

We agreed that our Opening Night will be on (date)_____, and this session will run until (date) _____.

Compatibility Survey

Heads of Household   _____

Address   _____

Phone   _____

Cell(s)   _____

E-mail(s)   _____

Today's Date   _____

This survey should be filled out by the chef of the house and then used as a guide to help communicate your style to prospective co-chefs.

In terms of my cooking and eating, I'd classify myself as (circle all that apply)

Betty Beginner
Omnivorous Thrill Seeker
Comfort Foodie
Vegetarian Wonder
Midwestern Mama
Carnivore
Fish-o-phile
1950s Throwback
Asian Maven
All-American
Lover of Light 'n' Healthy
Down-home Southern Cook
Organic Fanatic
Locavore
Other _____

With the right influences, I could also become (circle all that apply)

Iron Chef
Omnivorous Thrill Seeker
Comfort Foodie
Vegetarian Wonder
Midwestern Mama
Carnivore
Fish-o-phile
1950s Throwback
Asian Maven
All-American
Lover of Light 'n' Healthy
Organic Fanatic
Locavore
Other _____

My biggest goals in joining a dinner co-op would be_____
_____
_____.

Realistically, I can see my family enjoying weeknight dinners that _____ than we currently eat.
◯   include more meat
◯   include more vegetables
◯   include more variety
◯   other _____

My favorite local restaurants include_____.

www.dinnerco-ops.com

Compatibility Survey

My favorite celebrity chefs (if any) are_____.

My favorite cookbooks are_____.

In my kitchen, Parmesan cheese (check one)
- ○ is shaken from a green cylinder ○ is carefully shaved from an aged block
- ○ doesn't exist

At our house, garlic comes from (check one)
- ○ a jar ○ a shaker ○ a bulb with papery skin

Salad dressing is best (check all that apply)
- ○ before the "best before" date on the bottle ○ when made from scratch

Whether my kids will like what my co-chefs cook is (check one)
- ○ a consideration, but not as important as whether the adults will enjoy it
- ○ taken into account—they can try it but don't always have to like it
- ○ doesn't apply

Our family would like to cook and receive meat-based dinners (check one)
- ○ every night ○ most nights ○ some nights ○ no nights

Notes:

I would be happy cooking and receiving (check all options that you'd consider)
- ○ main entrée
- ○ main entrée plus a vegetable, salad, or fruit*
- ○ meals that include all three: vegetables, starch, and protein*
- ○ main entrée plus two sides and bread

*recommended

We need vegetables, salad, or fruit to be well represented

never   1   2   3   4   5   in every dinner

In terms of portion sizes, I'd say we eat like

baby birds   1   2   3   4   5   lumberjacks

When it comes to acceptable levels of fat and calories, I'm best described as
- ○ a zero-fat body Nazi
- ○ a pursuer of light and healthy meals that still taste good
- ○ a balance seeker—everything in moderation
- ○ someone who eats most any food that looks good and tastes good
- ○ a hedonist—butter me up
- ○ a strict dieter (please describe) _____

My special dietary needs include _____.

www.dinnerco-ops.com

Food Preferences

Name of family _____

Home phone _____

Circle the ingredients your family members are allergic to or strongly dislike. Try to eliminate as few ingredients as possible.

Meats & Fish
Bacon
Beef, ground
Beef, roast
Beef, steak
Chicken, dark
Chicken, white
Clams
Crab
Duck
Halibut
Ham
Italian sausage
Lamb
Liver
Lobster
Mussels
Oysters
Pork chops
Pork tenderloin
Prosciutto
Salmon
Scallops
Shrimp
Snapper
Swordfish
Tempeh
Tofu
Trout
Tuna, canned
Tuna, steak
Turkey
Turkey, ground

Dairy
Blue cheese
Brie
Buttermilk
Cheddar
Cottage cheese
Cream cheese
Feta
Goat Cheese
Gruyère
Ricotta
Sour cream
Swiss
Yogurt

Miscellaneous
Almonds
Capers
Cashews
Coconut
Mayonnaise
Miracle Whip
Olives
Peanut butter
Peanuts
Pecans
Pickles
Pine nuts
Walnuts

Grains & Beans
Barley
Black beans
Black-eyed peas
Bulgur
Falafel
Garbanzos
Hummus
Kidney beans
Lentils
Millet
Navy beans
Oatmeal
Polenta
Rice, basmati
Rice, brown
Rice noodles
Soy beans (Edamame)
Split peas

Food Preferences

Vegetables

Artichoke
Arugula
Asparagus
Beans, green
Beans, lima
Beets
Bok choy
Broccoli
Brussels sprouts
Cabbage
Carrots
Cauliflower
Corn
Cucumber
Eggplant
Greens:
  beet
  mustard
  other
Okra
Parsnip
Peas
Pepper, bell
Pepper, chile
Potatoes
Pumpkin
Radicchio
Rutabaga
Snow (snap) peas
Spinach
Squash, summer
Squash, winter
Sweet potato
Swiss chard
Tomato
Turnip

Fruits

Apple
Apricot
Avocado
Banana
Berries
Cantaloupe
Cherries
Cranberries
Dates
Figs
Grapefruit
Grapes
Mango
Nectarine
Orange
Papaya
Peach
Pear
Pineapple
Plums
Prunes
Raisins
Rhubarb
Tangerine

Herbs & Seasonings

Basil
Cilantro
Chile powder*
Cinnamon
Cumin
Curry
Dill
Fennel
Garlic
Parsley
Tarragon
Soy sauce
Sugar

Others

_____
_____
_____
_____
_____
_____

*Spicy or Mild?
What is your family's preferred level of spiciness?

When you buy salsa, do you usually buy (check all that apply)
○ mild
○ medium
○ hot
○ extra hot

www.dinnerco-ops.com

Food Safety Checklist

Nobody expects you to wear a hairnet. But as a group, let's agree to follow these safe practices:

Meal Preparation: Start clean and keep foods separate.

» Start with a clean sink and counters.

» Bring out clean kitchen towels, dish cloths, and a fresh apron.

» Wash hands frequently with hot water and soap.

» Keep meat and raw foods separate.

» Use separate cutting boards for meat and veggies/fruit.

» Prep raw fruits and vegetables before prepping meats and keep them separate.

» Defrost meats in the refrigerator or use microwave defrost settings and then refrigerate.

» Marinate meats in the refrigerator, covered. Separate out any marinade you might use later as a sauce before you start marinating. Discard any leftover marinade that has been in contact with meat.

Delivery: Keep hot foods hot and cold foods cold.

» Preheat serving dishes that hold hot food (in a low-temp oven if they're Pyrex).

» Chill serving dishes that hold cold food (Pyrex chills nicely).

» Fill serving dishes just before you're ready to deliver, or refrigerate and attach a note on how to reheat to serving temperature.

» Keep hot foods and cold foods separate by storing them in separate containers.

» Make arrangements with your members in case they're not at home when you deliver—an insulated cooler on a protected porch, a hidden key, or a garage code so you can put food right in their fridge.

Food safety—we get it.

Signed,

_____   _____
Your Co-Chef   Your Co-Chef

_____   _____
Your Co-Chef   Your Co-Chef

www.dinnerco-ops.com

Kick-Off Meeting Summary (Sample)

If the organizing chef has time, it's nice to compile and distribute the key information on one page after your kick-off meeting. You will also keep a more in-depth profile for each family.

North End Dinner Co-op

Goals: Eat better, save effort, discover new cuisine

Schedule:
Monday: Liz
Tuesday: Alex
Wednesday: Sarah

Delivery Guidelines:
Deliver between 5:30 and 6:00 p.m.
Always deliver 1 set (each set: one rectangle + one round) of containers
Meat, starch, and vegetable or fruit
3 portions/household
Homemade or prepared dressings included with salads

Foods to Avoid:
lima beans
coconut
trout
Miracle Whip
liver
excessive raw onion

Moderately spicy food is good.

Preferred doneness for meats:
Darin and Liz: Medium well
Gary and Alex: Medium rare/medium
Henry and Sarah: Medium rare

Favorite pizza:
Pepperoni and black olive
Zucchini Meany
Artichoke mushroom

Darin and Liz	4321 Thatcher Street	555-2354
Gary and Alex	9122 N. 8th Street	867-5309
Henry and Sarah	1234 N. 7th Street	555-5432

www.dinnerco-ops.com

Co-op Member Profile

Complete this profile of your household and distribute to your entire team for easy reference. Also provide copies to your spouses and partners in case of last-minute changes.

FAMILY

ADDRESS

HOME PHONE

HOME E-MAIL

CHEF

WORK #

CELL #

WORK E-MAIL   BIRTHDAY

PARTNER

WORK #

CELL #

WORK E-MAIL   BIRTHDAY

KIDS (IF ANY)

NAME   BIRTHDAY

NAME   BIRTHDAY

NAME   BIRTHDAY

Delivery instructions (on the mat, in a cooler, garage code, hidden key, pets to watch for):

Someone is usually home by _____.

Chef cooks on   M   T   W   TH   F

Preferred doneness for meat (circle one):
Rare   Medium-rare   Medium   Medium-well   Well-done

Favorite pizza order:

Session Evaluation Form

Name _____

Last session, our favorite meals from each chef were the following:

From Chef _____
Dinner _____
Why? _____

From Chef _____
Dinner _____
Why? _____

From Chef _____
Dinner _____
Why? _____

From Chef _____
Dinner _____
Why? _____

"No thank you" List
So many recipes, so little time—let's concentrate on the absolute favorites and continue to have fun trying new ones. Any recipes from this session you'd rather not see again?

Anything we should address as a group at this time?

Vacation Notice

Vacation Notice

We, _____ are going to be away from ___ /___ /___ to
___ /___ /___. This means we will think of you fondly but won't cook on
_____ or receive dinners on the following nights
_____.

◯ Your Guest Chef will be _____.

address _____
phone _____
cell _____
e-mail _____

or

◯ Please count us out during this time frame.

We'll see you when we get back from_____.
Questions? Call _____. Ta-ta!

Vacation Notice

We, _____are going to be away from ___ /___ /___ to
___ /___ /___. This means we will think of you fondly but won't cook on
_____ or receive dinners on the following nights
_____.

◯ Your Guest Chef will be _____.

address _____
phone _____
cell _____
e-mail _____

or

◯ Please count us out during this time frame.

We'll see you when we get back from_____.
Questions? Call _____. Ta-ta!

Kids Rave Reviews

Kids: Fill one of these out and hand it to the chef who made something good. Maybe they will make it again for you sometime soon.

Rave Review

Dear Chef _____,

I thought your _____ was absolutely

_____. What made it so good was the _____

_____.

Sincerely,

Rave Review

Dear Chef _____,,

I thought your _____ was absolutely

_____. What made it so good was the _____

_____.

Sincerely,

www.dinnerco-ops.com

Acknowledgments

Like a great dinner co-op, this book is a product of the enthusiasm and contributions of several cooks who've shared their recipe feedback, advice, and anecdotes. Many of them live in the North End and East End neighborhoods of Boise, Idaho, where new dinner co-ops pop up like wild mushrooms.

We are hugely grateful to our committed team of recipe testers: Debbie Dakins, Sarah Woodley, Holly Ponath, Janet Parsons, Lee Honsinger, Vida Lietuvninkas, Jennifer Stevens, Jen Dyer, and Rejane Kocemba, along with Judy Wilbur, Sheila Grisham, Kelli Chavez, Kim Smith-Fausset, Gary Davis, Kristy Weyhrich, Uma & Irwin Mulnick, Jan Bethke, and Sandy Parks.

Thank you to our own dear families for your incredible support: Gary, Mae, and Adele Davis, Paul and Jesse Remeis, and Michael Ellis. And to Tony & Judy Wilbur, Karen Penafiel, Walter Remeis, Max & Gloria Dakins, Debbie Dakins, all the Dakinses, John Regis, Jock & Monica Heckman, Elsa Heckman McMakin, Pat Davis, Ann Shaffer, and all the Heckmans, Davises, and Carrascos. And to Terra Bourguignon, Jennifer Casey, Sandy Parks, Chrissy Bowers, Jane Williamson, and Deb Nicholson. For two years you called to ask, "How's the book going?" We love you for that.

We'd like to thank the families in our own dinner co-ops, who never grew tired of our quest: the Grishams, the Sims-Lanes, the Woodleys, the Bowers-Stecklers, the Parks, the Stevens, Don Gura and Vida Lietuvninkas, the Shadle-Browns, and Liz and Darin Weyhrich. We wish you continued dinnertime bliss.

We so appreciate the gifted photographer Deborah Hardee, the brilliant Kristy Weyhrich of W Design, and our food stylist Lance Reynolds of Open Road Design. Thank you to our agent Katherine Fausset for helping connect us with great partners. We thank our editor, Katie Newbold, whose last name says it all. And Suzanne Taylor of Gibbs Smith, who gets it.

For reasons they understand, we are grateful to Dr. Waj Nasser, Don and Theresa Burkes, Chelle Nystrom, Don and Patrice Childres, Julie Robinson, A. J. Eaton, Michele Franco Koehl, Bryan Escobedo, actress Hollis Welsh, Deana Chandler, actress Amy Gile, Dan Misner, and Eric Barth. Thanks to Drew and Suzanne McDaniel at Impact Imports, Robbye Clements at Scandia Down, Roger Phillips, Russ Stoddard, Susan Rowe, Morgan Hill, Stan Heinz, Corey Cruz, Zachary Stevens, Sue Jones, Gloria Brewer, Julie Gray with Bobbi Brown, Casey Berliner, David Jenson, and April VanDeGrift from the Boise Co-op. From Gibbs Smith, we thank Melissa Dymock, Renee Wald, and our publicist Jamie Moio.

Thanks to all of you, we had an absolute blast making this book.

Index